Section Four — Writing Techniques

Section Five — Exam Techniques

Section Six — The Exam

Section Seven — Sample Answers

Published by CGP

Editors:
Joe Brazier
Charley Darbishire
Mary Falkner
Katherine Reed
Edward Robinson
Caley Simpson
Jennifer Underwood

Contributors:
Caroline Bagshaw
Lorraine Campbell
Graham Fletcher
Jane Harrison
Nicola Woodfin

ISBN: 978 1 84146 760 3

With thanks to Heather Gregson and John Sanders for the proofreading.
With thanks to Laura Stoney for the copyright research.

Groovy website: www.cgpbooks.co.uk
Jolly bits of clipart from CorelDRAW®
Printed by Elanders Ltd, Newcastle upon Tyne.

Based on the classic CGP style created by Richard Parsons.

How to Use This Book

This book will help you do better in <u>Section A</u> of your <u>Unit 1 exam</u> for <u>GCSE English</u> or <u>GCSE English Language</u>. This part of the exam is on "Understanding non-fiction texts", which can mean newspaper and magazine articles, travel writing, adverts, biographies — basically anything that's not made up.

The Assessment Objectives tell you what Skills you need

The <u>assessment objectives</u> are the things that AQA says you need to be able to do to get <u>good marks</u> for this part of the exam. Don't worry — there aren't very many of them. Put simply, you have to:

1) <u>Understand</u> what a text is <u>telling you</u> and use good <u>quotes</u> as <u>evidence</u> for your points. You'll also have to <u>compare</u> texts by looking for similarities and differences between them, and use appropriate <u>examples</u> to back up your points.

2) Explain how writers use <u>language</u>, <u>grammar</u>, <u>layout</u> and <u>structure</u> to make their writing <u>effective</u>, and say how <u>effective</u> you think a text is in getting its <u>message</u> across to the <u>reader</u>.

Each Section of the book deals with a Different Skill

SECTION 1 discusses the <u>audience</u> (who the author is writing for) and the <u>purpose</u> (why they're writing). There are examples of different kinds of <u>non-fiction texts</u> and how to write about them.

SECTION 2 has plenty of tips on how to <u>follow an argument</u> and how to write about one. It explains the techniques that writers use to <u>argue a point</u>, and how they work.

SECTION 3 is about the <u>presentation</u> and <u>layout</u> of texts — how the way they <u>look</u> affects how they come across to the reader.

SECTION 4 is all about <u>writing techniques</u> — how writers use different <u>styles of writing</u>, <u>language techniques</u> and <u>structure</u> to make their work more effective.

SECTION 5 gives you loads of <u>tips</u> on what you can do in the <u>exam</u> to get <u>great marks</u>.

SECTION 6 contains a <u>mock exam</u>, so you know what the real thing will look like.

SECTION 7 shows you the <u>mark scheme</u> for the mock exam in Section 6. Then there are loads of <u>sample answers</u>, working up from a <u>C grade</u> to the famous <u>A*</u>.

At the end of the book there's a handy <u>glossary</u> that gives you <u>definitions</u> of loads of important <u>words and terms</u> that you might need.

The book also doubles up as a rather fetching hat...

This book is full of straightforward ways of getting <u>extra marks</u>. Read through the explanations and examples and practise all the tips individually. Then try to include as many as you can in your work.

The Audience

When you're reading a non-fiction text, you've got to think about the <u>audience</u> — the people that the writer wants to read their work.

Writers aim their work at a Specific Audience

The writer will always have a <u>specific group of people</u> in mind as their audience when they write.

e.g.

TEXT	AUDIENCE
Article in 'The Financial Times'	Business people
Travel guide book	Holiday-makers
Problem page in 'Sugar'	Teenage girls

Some texts will have more than one audience, e.g. toy adverts will try to appeal to the kids who use them but also to the parents who have to buy them.

Content and Form can show who the audience is

1) Sometimes you can work out who the audience is by the text's <u>content</u> (subject matter), e.g. an article in 'Top Gear' magazine about cars is obviously aimed at someone who's into cars.

2) The <u>form</u> (the way a text is <u>laid out</u>) can also tell you who the intended audience is. E.g. a <u>large font</u> and lots of <u>pictures</u> means it's probably for children, but if there's lots of text crammed into <u>dense columns</u>, it's more likely to be intended for adults.

Betty often bought "Top Gear" for herself, and "Medieval Role Play" for Bert.

Language can give you plenty of clues too

1) The <u>vocabulary</u> (choice of words) can tell you about the target audience, e.g. about the <u>age group</u>:

> Today, we witnessed a discussion on fox-hunting. As one can imagine, this issue, although it has been debated for many years, still managed to elicit mixed emotions from all concerned.

Difficult vocabulary, e.g. saying 'elicit' rather than just 'bring out', and complex sentences show this text is aimed at adults.

> Dungeon Killer 3 is the hottest new game of the year! There are 52 amazing levels and 6 cool new characters — don't miss out on the wildest gaming experience of your life!

Modern slang and simple sentences show this is aimed at younger people.

2) The language can also give you clues about the target audience's <u>level of understanding</u>:

> The object of a game of football is to get the ball in the opposing team's goal. Sounds easy, doesn't it? Well, firstly, the other team has the same thing in mind. Secondly, there are eleven of them who are trying to stop you.

Simple, general explanations show this is for beginners.

> The next hole was a par-3 and I hit my tee shot directly onto the green. Sadly my putting let me down badly and I ended up getting a bogey.

Technical vocabulary shows this is for people who know a bit about the sport.

Hello? Is there anybody there?

You need to work out who the intended audience is so that you can discuss the writer's intentions, techniques, and how successful they are. Keep the audience in mind throughout your answer.

The Purpose of the Text

Another big thing you need to work out about the text you get in the exam is: "What is the writer's <u>purpose</u>?" In other words, "<u>Why</u> has the writer written this?" Why indeed.

There are four Common Purposes of writing

The <u>purpose</u> of the text means the <u>reason</u> that it has been written — what the writer is <u>trying to do</u>. All non-fiction texts are written for <u>one or more</u> of these reasons:

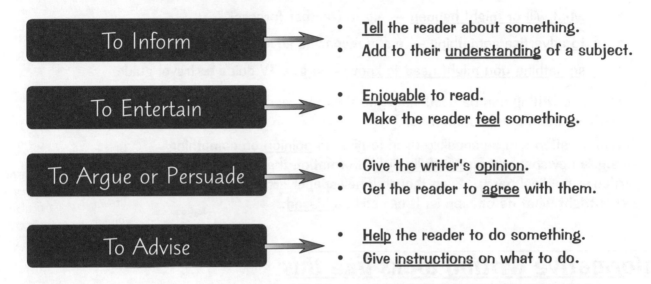

| To Inform | → | • <u>Tell</u> the reader about something.
 • Add to their <u>understanding</u> of a subject. |

| To Entertain | → | • <u>Enjoyable</u> to read.
 • Make the reader <u>feel</u> something. |

| To Argue or Persuade | → | • Give the writer's <u>opinion</u>.
 • Get the reader to <u>agree</u> with them. |

| To Advise | → | • <u>Help</u> the reader to do something.
 • Give <u>instructions</u> on what to do. |

Pages 4-7 tell you how to spot which of these purposes the writer has in mind, and how you can <u>discuss</u> them in the exam.

Tone and Style are closely related

1) In the same way that there are different <u>tones of voice</u> when people speak, e.g. calm, angry, friendly, there are different <u>tones</u> that writers can use — see pages 10-11.

2) <u>Style</u> is to do with the type of language and techniques a writer uses, for example formal or informal — see pages 8-9.

3) Writers choose a style and tone that's appropriate for the <u>audience</u> they're writing for and the <u>purpose</u> of writing.

> When you're reading a non-fiction text, remember to think about:
> * <u>who</u> the author is writing for (audience)
> * what they're <u>trying to do</u> (purpose)
> * <u>how</u> they write (style and tone)
> * how much you think they <u>succeed</u>.

WARNING: Being too informal can lead to dire consequences.

My life has no purpose — but I do have a dog that barks...

Some texts have more than one purpose, e.g. travel books are generally meant to entertain, as they're full of interesting little stories, but they're usually informative too, as they tell you great places to go where you won't meet other tourists — unless they've read the book as well, that is.

Informative Texts

If the purpose of a text is to <u>inform</u> you, the writer's aim is to pass on knowledge to you as clearly and effectively as possible. Informative texts have lots of <u>facts</u> and usually a <u>straightforward style</u>.

Informative Writing Tells You something

1) Informative texts give the reader <u>facts and information</u>. This could be:

   - <u>what has happened</u> — e.g. a bank statement or a history book

   - <u>what will or might happen</u> — e.g. a weather forecast

   - <u>to advertise something</u> — e.g. a magazine advert or a brochure

   - <u>something you might need to know</u> — e.g. a **TV** guide or travel guide

2) Informative writing can be used simply to help the reader <u>understand</u> something, as in a school textbook.

3) But information can be sneakily used to give an <u>opinion</u> on something — e.g. a newspaper may <u>carefully pick</u> information that supports a particular political party. Even though a newspaper article may not say outright what its opinion is, it can still be <u>biased</u>.

Bias is when the writer's own opinions affect their writing, so that it leans towards a particular opinion — see page 19.

Informative Writing looks like this

Gives you specific details and dates.

The Mini first went on sale in 1959. It soon became the best selling car in Europe. Over five million of them were made and many famous people, including The Beatles, bought them.

The Mini Cooper S version won the Monte Carlo Rally in 1964. Minis were less expensive than many other cars. Now they are made by BMW and aimed at a different market.

There were moments when Hank regretted buying a cheap and affordable car.

Contains facts rather than opinions.

Write about informative texts Like This

Make a clear opening point.

Use quotes to back up your points.

Build on your ideas.

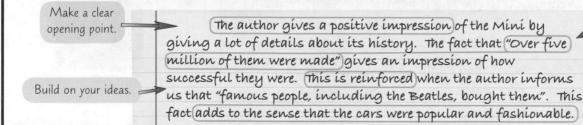

The author gives a positive impression of the Mini by giving a lot of details about its history. The fact that "Over five million of them were made" gives an impression of how successful they were. This is reinforced when the author informs us that "famous people, including the Beatles, bought them". This fact adds to the sense that the cars were popular and fashionable.

Explain the effect of the quote.

If there are lots of facts and figures, it's informative

You need to show you can recognise informative writing and explain how it's used. Don't assume it's obvious — spell out to the examiner exactly what the writer is informing us about, why they're doing it and how effective you think they are. Make sure you point out if the information is biased.

Entertaining Texts

Entertaining texts means writing that you would read for <u>pleasure</u>. There are less of the cold, hard (and sometimes a teeny bit dull) facts of informative writing and more of the kind of things that make you <u>scared</u>, <u>excited</u> or <u>amused</u>. That's more of the fun stuff, then...

Entertaining Writing aims to be Enjoyable to read

1) Entertaining writing is meant to be <u>interesting</u>. People read it mostly for <u>fun</u> (although they might <u>learn</u> something at the same time). Travel books are a good example of entertaining non-fiction writing.

2) The author might entertain the reader with <u>anecdotes</u> (stories of <u>funny things</u> that happened to them). Or they might use <u>entertaining descriptions and comparisons</u> of things or people.

3) Entertaining writing has more <u>creative</u> and <u>unexpected</u> bits than informative writing.

Entertaining Writing looks like this

This piece of writing is on the same subject as the one on page 4 — but this one is <u>entertaining</u>. Have a look at how it's different from the informative one.

> My first car was a 1970 Mini. I loved it from the moment I sat in it. It went like a rocket. By that I mean it always had smoke coming out of its rear end! Perhaps I shouldn't have tried to drive it like Michael Caine.
>
> It was a subtle shade of bright orange and should have come complete with free executive sunglasses. Still, I was a student then and they wouldn't have fitted my image.

Interesting similes and comparisons.

Contains funny images.

Tells a story.

Write about entertaining texts Like This

Make an opening point.

The author gains the reader's attention by using the first person ("I") in her writing. That makes her experiences seem more real. She uses humour to maintain interest. For example "It always had smoke coming out of its rear end!" paints an entertaining picture and the exclamation mark reinforces the effect of the joke. The comical contrast of "subtle shade" and "bright orange" helped me to visualise the car and enjoy the description.

Use evidence from the text.

Give a personal reaction — this shows you're enthusiastic about it.

Nobby found the new Bill Bryson book most entertaining.

Writing exam answers — now that's texertainment...

Some texts will be both informative and entertaining, e.g. a travel book may contain useful facts about a place but also give you some funny anecdotes about what happened when the author was there. Try to work out which bits of the text inform and which entertain when you write about them.

Texts that Argue or Persuade

One purpose of writing is to <u>argue</u> a point, to get the reader to agree with it. This purpose is very common in exam texts. Some texts go a stage further and try to <u>persuade</u> you to actually do something, like donate money to save a rare species of hamster, or something like that anyway.

Arguing and Persuading are similar

1) When people write to <u>argue</u>, they want to make the reader <u>agree with their opinion</u>. They try to write <u>clearly</u> and <u>forcibly</u> to get their points across, e.g. newspaper editorials. At the end, the reader should not be in any doubt about what the writer's opinion is.

2) Sometimes writers try to <u>persuade</u> you to do something, e.g. to support a charity. This kind of writing will also be very <u>clear</u> and <u>open</u> about its aims and opinions.

Writing to Argue looks like this

Statistics used to back up argument.

Separate paragraph increases impact of last line.

People who claim that young people are lazy are guilty of both prejudice and ignorance. The vast majority are anything but lazy. In a recent survey of 14-16 year olds, 76% said they had a Saturday job and another 6% did weekday paper rounds.

Does that sound like laziness to you?

Opinions clear from the start.

Rhetorical question (see p.18) challenges the reader to think about the issue.

Persuasive writing looks like this

Direct, opinionated tone.

Makes a direct personal appeal to the reader.

Young workers have been shamelessly exploited by greedy employers for far too long. It's time that this disgraceful situation was changed. Each and every one of us should take responsibility for making sure that our young people get the fair treatment that they deserve.
By signing our petition you can send a message to the government — that people under 18 are hard-working, and just as deserving of decent pay and a safe working environment as everyone else.

Uses emotive language, e.g. greedy.

Clearly states what the reader should do.

Write about texts that argue or persuade Like This

Work small quotes into your answer.

The writer argues his point very forcefully. He uses statistics to show that many young people have jobs and accuses those who disagree with him of "prejudice and ignorance". This suggests that anyone who thinks young people are lazy has not really thought the issue through.

Show how the writer's argument works.

Persuasive texts are great, don't you agree? Yes you do...

If a writer is trying to argue a point or persuade you to do something, it's all about getting the reader to see things from their point of view. It won't be balanced, like a discussion — it'll be one-sided, with evidence that's carefully chosen because it supports their point of view.

Texts that Advise

When people write to advise, they're trying to help the reader to <u>do something</u>, or to make the right <u>decision</u>. The style is clearer and less emotional than writing that argues or persuades.

Writing to Advise sounds Clear and Calm

1) When people are writing to advise, they want their readers to <u>follow their suggestions</u>.

2) The tone will be <u>calm</u> and <u>less emotional</u> than writing that argues or persuades.

3) The advice will usually be <u>clearly written and laid out</u>. The writer may use bullet points or numbered lists to make it easier to follow.

4) The style may be <u>formal</u>, e.g. in a letter from your bank offering financial advice, or <u>informal</u>, e.g. in a magazine advice column (see pages 8-9).

> <u>Instructive texts</u> are texts that give you advice on something very specific in a step-by-step way — like assembly instructions for furniture.

"Congratulations on purchasing your new TS-522/A shell..."

Writing to Advise looks like this

Addresses the reader by using "you".

> Before you buy a pension, you need to be sure that it is the right one for you — dropping out can mean that you lose a lot of the money you've already paid in. You should look at the pension company's reputation, past results and penalties for changing schemes.

Friendly warning.

Uses specific details to give practical advice.

Write about texts that advise Like This

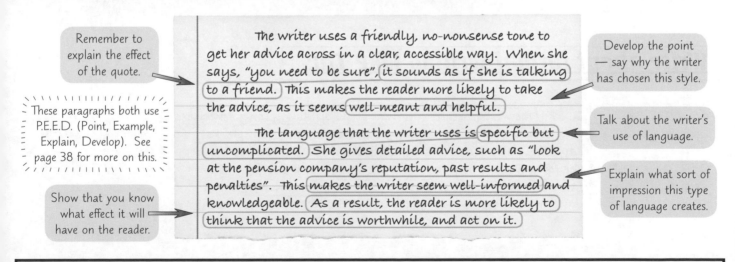

Remember to explain the effect of the quote.

These paragraphs both use P.E.E.D. (Point, Example, Explain, Develop). See page 38 for more on this.

Show that you know what effect it will have on the reader.

The writer uses a friendly, no-nonsense tone to get her advice across in a clear, accessible way. When she says, "you need to be sure", it sounds as if she is talking to a friend. This makes the reader more likely to take the advice, as it seems well-meant and helpful.

The language that the writer uses is specific but uncomplicated. She gives detailed advice, such as "look at the pension company's reputation, past results and penalties". This makes the writer seem well-informed and knowledgeable. As a result, the reader is more likely to think that the advice is worthwhile, and act on it.

Develop the point — say why the writer has chosen this style.

Talk about the writer's use of language.

Explain what sort of impression this type of language creates.

Texts that advise are clearly presented and easy to follow

Texts that advise generally assume you're already on the writer's side — people usually choose to read them because they want to know about something and they trust the writer's opinion. Because of this, they usually sound more friendly and less "in-your-face" than texts that argue or persuade.

Formal Style

Formal <u>writing</u> is writing that sounds polite or "<u>correct</u>" — the sort of writing you use in schoolwork.
<u>Informal writing</u> is the opposite — a <u>relaxed</u> casual style, like the way you'd write to your mates.

There are a few ways of Spotting Formal Writing

1) It's quite easy to recognise a formal style of writing. Just think about the way a <u>letter from your teacher</u> or a <u>newspaper article</u> would be written.

2) Here are a few common <u>features</u> of formal writing:

> • a dry or "stuffy" tone (not exciting or emotional)
> • standard English — no slang or abbreviations
> • long sentences with correct punctuation
> • sounds impersonal — the writer doesn't try to relate to you

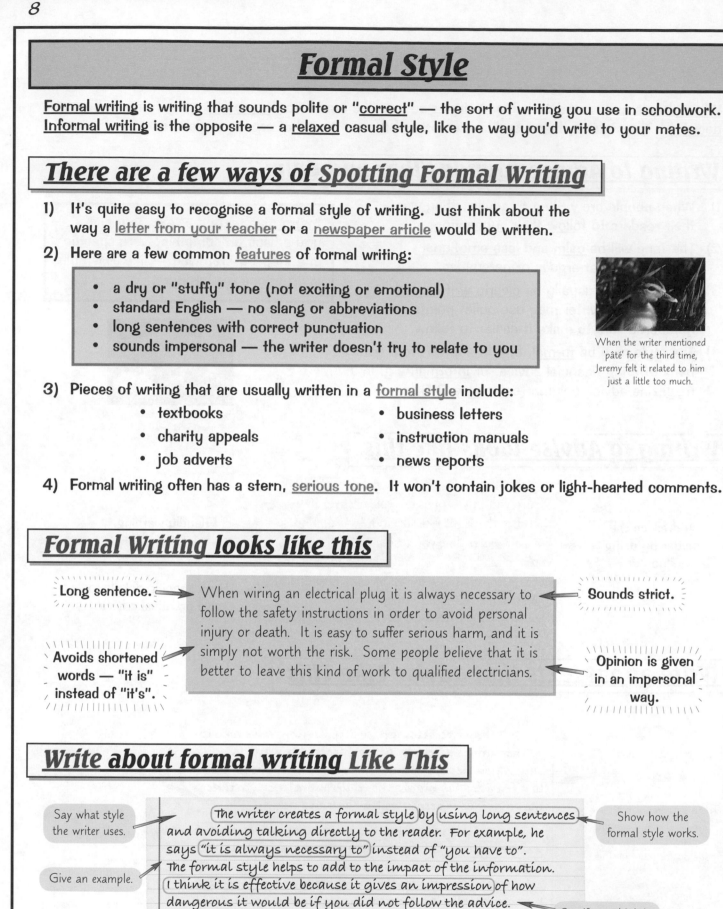

When the writer mentioned 'pâté' for the third time, Jeremy felt it related to him just a little too much.

3) Pieces of writing that are usually written in a <u>formal style</u> include:

> • textbooks
> • charity appeals
> • job adverts

> • business letters
> • instruction manuals
> • news reports

4) Formal writing often has a stern, <u>serious tone</u>. It won't contain jokes or light-hearted comments.

Formal Writing looks like this

Long sentence.

Avoids shortened words — "it is" instead of "it's".

> When wiring an electrical plug it is always necessary to follow the safety instructions in order to avoid personal injury or death. It is easy to suffer serious harm, and it is simply not worth the risk. Some people believe that it is better to leave this kind of work to qualified electricians.

Sounds strict.

Opinion is given in an impersonal way.

Write about formal writing Like This

Say what style the writer uses.

Give an example.

> The writer creates a formal style by using long sentences and avoiding talking directly to the reader. For example, he says "it is always necessary to" instead of "you have to". The formal style helps to add to the impact of the information. I think it is effective because it gives an impression of how dangerous it would be if you did not follow the advice.

Show how the formal style works.

Say if you think it works and why.

One is undoubtedly required to discuss formal writing...

Basically, if a text sounds like it's been written by a teacher or a bank manager, it's formal. As usual, you need to say why the writer has chosen to use this style — think about who they're writing for and what message they're trying to give, and say how the formal style helps them do this.

Informal Style

Informal writing sounds as if someone is <u>chatting</u> to you. It sounds more <u>friendly</u> and <u>casual</u> than formal writing. Writers often use an informal style to try to build up a <u>relationship</u> with the reader.

Informal Writing sounds chatty

1) If writing is clearly <u>not formal</u>, it's — wait for it — <u>informal</u>. Tricky eh?

2) Here are a few common <u>features</u> of informal writing:

- chatty comments, as if the writer is talking to you
- non-standard English — e.g. abbreviations and slang
- short, simple sentences
- jokes and a light-hearted tone

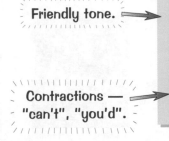

Light-hearted Tone was a perfect match for Carefree Meg.

3) Pieces of writing that are often written in an <u>informal style</u> include:

- teenage magazine articles
- adverts aimed at young people
- gossip columns
- travel writing

Informal Writing looks like this

Friendly tone.

Contractions — "can't", "you'd".

So, you want to wire a plug? Well, take my advice and follow the instructions. Being a bright spark is one thing but you don't want to end up that way permanently, do you? Have a go if you must, but don't take risks. If you can't do it, you'd be better off letting somebody who knows their way around electrics do it for you.

Light-hearted comments.

Uses "you" and "my" — sounds personal.

Write about informal writing Like This

Use an example for every point.

The writer's informal opening, "So", makes the reader feel as if he is talking to them. This is added to by the use of abbreviations like "you'd" and "don't" which are usually used more in speech than writing.

Slang phrases such as "bright spark" and "knows their way around" give the impression that the writer is just an ordinary person. By using humour like "you don't want to end up that way permanently, do you?", the writer makes an important point without seeming too serious.

Say how the language makes it sound informal.

Show how the informal style works.

Informal writing helps the reader relate to the writer...

The formality or informality of a piece of writing is all about the way it's expressed, rather than what it actually says. Remember to explain who the writing is aimed at, what the writer is trying to do, how the writer is trying to do it, and how well you think the writer has done it.

Personal Tone

The differences between personal and impersonal writing are again all to do with the <u>style of writing</u>. Personal writing sounds like the author is <u>talking to you</u>, while impersonal writing, er... doesn't.

Personal Writing sounds like it's talking to you

1) Personal writing is written in the <u>first person</u> — it uses "I", "me", "my" etc.

2) The writing is all from the <u>writer's point of view</u>. It's as if the author is talking to you.

3) Because it's from the writer's point of view, it's often <u>biased</u> — it expresses the author's <u>personal opinions</u>, rather than being neutral.

4) Personal writing often expresses the author's <u>emotions</u>, e.g. fear, happiness, optimism, and can be <u>self-mocking</u> (where the author takes the mickey out of themselves).

5) An <u>informal style</u> of writing (see page 9) can be used to create a personal tone.

Personal Writing looks like this

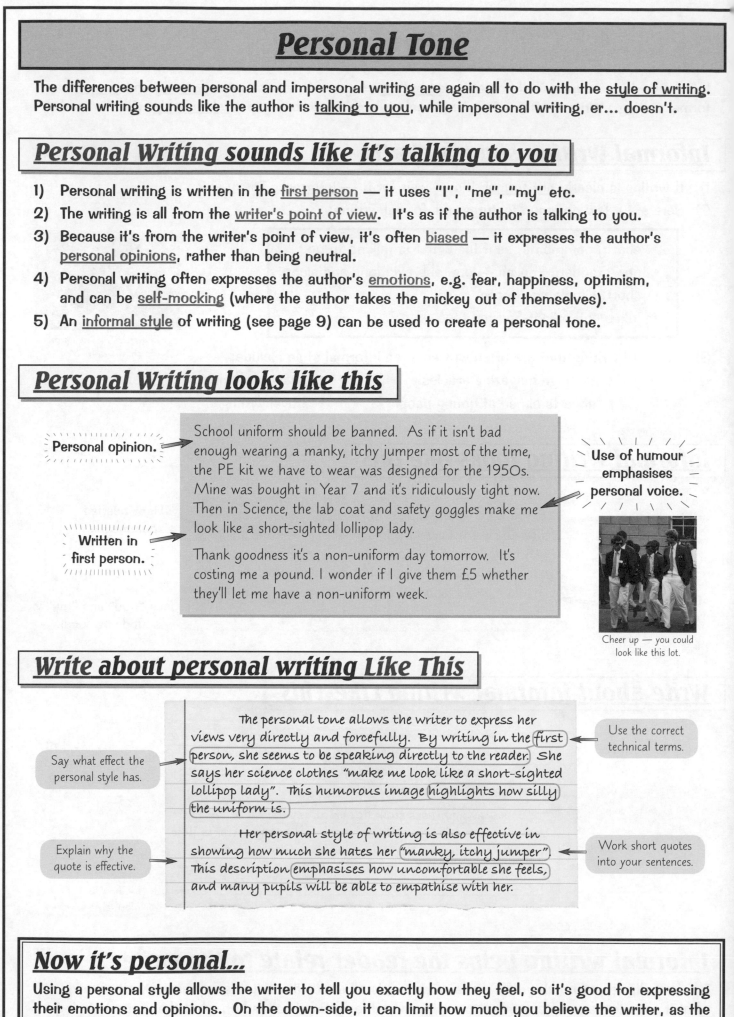

Personal opinion.

Written in first person.

School uniform should be banned. As if it isn't bad enough wearing a manky, itchy jumper most of the time, the PE kit we have to wear was designed for the 1950s. Mine was bought in Year 7 and it's ridiculously tight now. Then in Science, the lab coat and safety goggles make me look like a short-sighted lollipop lady.

Thank goodness it's a non-uniform day tomorrow. It's costing me a pound. I wonder if I give them £5 whether they'll let me have a non-uniform week.

Use of humour emphasises personal voice.

Cheer up — you could look like this lot.

Write about personal writing Like This

Say what effect the personal style has.

Explain why the quote is effective.

The personal tone allows the writer to express her views very directly and forcefully. By writing in the first person, she seems to be speaking directly to the reader. She says her science clothes "make me look like a short-sighted lollipop lady". This humorous image highlights how silly the uniform is.

Her personal style of writing is also effective in showing how much she hates her "manky, itchy jumper". This description emphasises how uncomfortable she feels, and many pupils will be able to empathise with her.

Use the correct technical terms.

Work short quotes into your sentences.

Now it's personal...

Using a personal style allows the writer to tell you exactly how they feel, so it's good for expressing their emotions and opinions. On the down-side, it can limit how much you believe the writer, as the reader is aware that it's very clearly just one person's opinion — you're unlikely to take it all as fact.

Impersonal Tone

With impersonal writing, the writer is <u>separate</u> from what they're writing about. There's no "I" or "we" — you're just told "this is what's going on", and it's presented as fact rather than opinion.

Impersonal Writing sounds Neutral and Detached

1) Impersonal writing is written in the <u>third person</u> — it uses "she", "him", "they" etc.

2) You don't get a sense of the writer's personality — it's as if it's written by an observer who is completely detached — <u>separate</u> from what's happening.

3) There's usually a <u>neutral tone</u> — the writer doesn't seem to be taking sides. But it can still be biased — the writer might quote <u>other people's opinions</u>, or they might sneakily say what they think but make out that it's a fact.

4) Impersonal writing sounds <u>unemotional</u> and <u>factual</u>.

5) A <u>formal style</u> of writing (see p.8) often creates an impersonal tone, e.g. in textbooks and job adverts.

Impersonal Writing looks like this

> Many pupils do not like school uniform. Perhaps this is not surprising as it is often identical to that worn by their grandparents in the 1950s. Uniforms can be expensive — especially if schools require them to be bought from specific retailers.
>
> Most young people would rather wear their own clothes so it is not unusual to find that non-uniform days are enthusiastically supported.

Neutral tone — doesn't sound opinionated.

Opinion disguised as fact.

Write about impersonal writing Like This

The writer uses an impersonal tone to give a negative impression of school uniforms. Factual comments like "Uniforms can be expensive" make the writer seem well-informed and also neutral. This adds strength to the idea that school uniforms are unpopular and unfair. However, the writer is clearly biased as these facts are very carefully chosen — no positive points are put forward for the wearing of uniforms.

Make a clear opening point.

Comment on the use of language.

Show you understand what the writer's up to.

Remember to use the P.E.E.D. method — see page 38.

Work out what impression the writer tries to give...

Watch out for writers who at first seem to be neutral. Even if they don't say "this is my opinion", they can still try to give a particular impression of something. Impersonal writing can be just as opinionated as personal writing — it's just a different way of presenting the writer's ideas.

Features of an Argument

If you're going to talk about a writer's argument in your answer, the first thing you need to do is <u>follow</u> the argument — in other words, <u>understand what points they're making</u>.

Look out for the Main Features of an Argument

A writer can use lots of different <u>techniques</u> when they argue a point. These might include:

* <u>facts</u> — see page 14.
* <u>opinions</u> — either the author's or someone else's. See page 15.
* <u>implications</u> — where the writer suggests something is the case without saying it outright, e.g. "Ever since Kelvin moved in, things have started mysteriously disappearing."
* <u>generalisations</u>, <u>rhetoric</u>, <u>counter-arguments</u> and <u>bias</u> — see pages 16-19.

All of these can be used either very obviously and deliberately, or more subtly. When you're following an argument, you have to spot <u>when</u> one of these turns up in the text, and say what <u>effect</u> it has.

Identify the Key Points of the argument

To follow an argument, you need to identify the <u>key points</u> — the main reasons the writer gives to back up their argument.

You can often spot where one key point ends and another one begins by the writer's use of <u>paragraphs</u>. A new paragraph often means a new key point:

In this increasingly stressful age it is important that young people find the time to relax and enjoy the best years of their life. With exam after exam, modern teenagers hardly have time to take a break and have fun with their friends.

The key point of the first paragraph is that schoolwork can prevent teenagers from enjoying themselves.

On top of the gruelling demands from school, the attitudes of well-meaning but demanding parents often do not help. The constant query of "Have you done your biology revision yet?" can only add to the stress and frustration of having to give up the opportunity of fun for more schoolwork.

The second paragraph moves onto a related but different point — the problems caused by parents.

Another way of spotting where a new point starts is when you see <u>linking words and phrases</u>:

| however | secondly | furthermore | on the other hand | in addition |

Taxi! Follow that argument...

If you try to talk about the whole text in one go, you'll more than likely end up in a sticky mess on the floor. But if you break an argument down into its main points, you'll find it a lot easier to discuss how the writer makes their points and how effective they are — see next page...

Evaluating an Argument

Evaluating an argument means saying how <u>effective</u> it is. You need to say whether or not you think it will successfully persuade the reader to agree with the writer, and why.

Say What's Good about the argument

1) It's <u>not enough</u> just to say an argument is good. You need to say <u>how</u> the writer makes their points and <u>why</u> they're effective.

2) Think about what kind of <u>impression</u> (e.g. forceful, emotional, knowledgeable) the writer creates with the language they use, and <u>how</u> this impression helps to <u>persuade</u> the reader.

Unfortunately this isn't the key to a good answer.

Evaluate an argument Like This

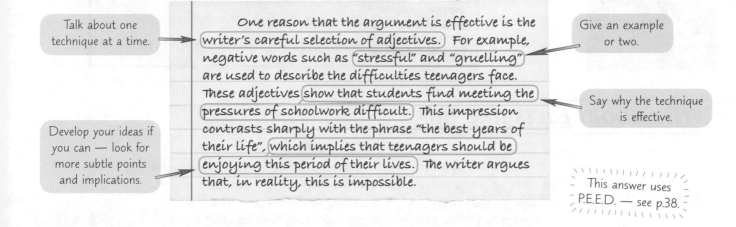

Talk about one technique at a time.

One reason that the argument is effective is the writer's careful selection of adjectives. For example, negative words such as "stressful" and "gruelling" are used to describe the difficulties teenagers face. These adjectives show that students find meeting the pressures of schoolwork difficult. This impression contrasts sharply with the phrase "the best years of their life", which implies that teenagers should be enjoying this period of their lives. The writer argues that, in reality, this is impossible.

Give an example or two.

Say why the technique is effective.

Develop your ideas if you can — look for more subtle points and implications.

This answer uses P.E.E.D. — see p.38.

The argument might have some Drawbacks

You might think some parts of an argument aren't convincing, and if that's what you reckon, <u>say so</u>. But if you do say this, make sure you've got some darn good <u>reasons</u> for saying so — if you just say, "the writer's argument is really stupid, he's missed the point", you won't get good marks.

Here are some criticisms you might be able to make:

1) <u>Inconsistencies</u> — sometimes a writer says things that contradict each other.

2) <u>Inaccuracies</u> — the writer's information might just be plain <u>wrong</u>. Watch out though — you have to really know your stuff before you go saying a point is inaccurate.

3) <u>Dullness</u> — sometimes an argument just won't grab you. This might be because it's <u>full of statistics</u> and not much else, or because the text is <u>confusing</u> or <u>unclear</u>. As always, if you can give examples of this, you'll pick up marks.

It was terrible! It wasn't that bad! It was great! MORE!

In your exam, you might be given a text that's presenting an argument. You need to be able to analyse the text by evaluating the argument and saying how successful it is. It's usually easiest to say mostly good things, but try to include one or two criticisms too, to make your answer balanced.

Facts

In your exam, it'll be useful if you can <u>spot facts and opinions</u> in texts and say what <u>effect</u> they have. Best get your head around the <u>difference</u> between them then...

Facts are definitely True...

FACT: Manchester United won the UEFA Champions League in May 2008.

FACT: Two metres of string is longer than one metre of string.

FACT: Barack Obama was the President of the United States after George W. Bush.

...apart from False Facts — they're Untrue

My degree in accountancy really helped me further my career at Oceanworld.

False facts are things that can be <u>proved</u> to be <u>untrue</u>, like these:

FALSE FACT: My nose is fifteen centimetres long.

FALSE FACT: Madonna's real name is Derek Tyson.

Write about Facts like this...

Make your point.

This answer uses P.E.E.D. — see p. 38.

You could use "for example" to start your examples — it makes it dead clear to the examiner what you're doing.

The author uses facts in the text to strengthen his argument that Carl Lewis is the greatest sprinter and long jumper in history. For example, he mentions Lewis's nine Olympic gold medals, two world records for the 100 metres, and 65 consecutive long jump competition victories. Each fact is evidence of Lewis' great success, adding weight to the author's case. However, I think the author's argument could be improved by comparing Carl Lewis to other successful sprinters and long-jumpers.

Explain why the author has used facts.

Develop your point.

Not like this...

Any fool can count the facts and say where they are. It's a <u>classic mistake</u>. Don't do it.

This answer is poor because it doesn't say how the facts help the writer's argument.

The author uses four facts in this text. There are two on line 2 and another two on line 5. He thinks that Carl Lewis is the greatest sprinter and long-jumper in the history of athletics.

Quote the facts — don't just say where they are like this answer does.

1 ———— 2

"Line 1 is longer than line 2" — fact, false fact or opinion...?

FACT — gorillas are hairier than slugs...

...except bald gorillas of course. Anyway, make sure you can spot the facts in a piece of text, and say how the author uses them to get their point across. Then go and shave a gorilla.

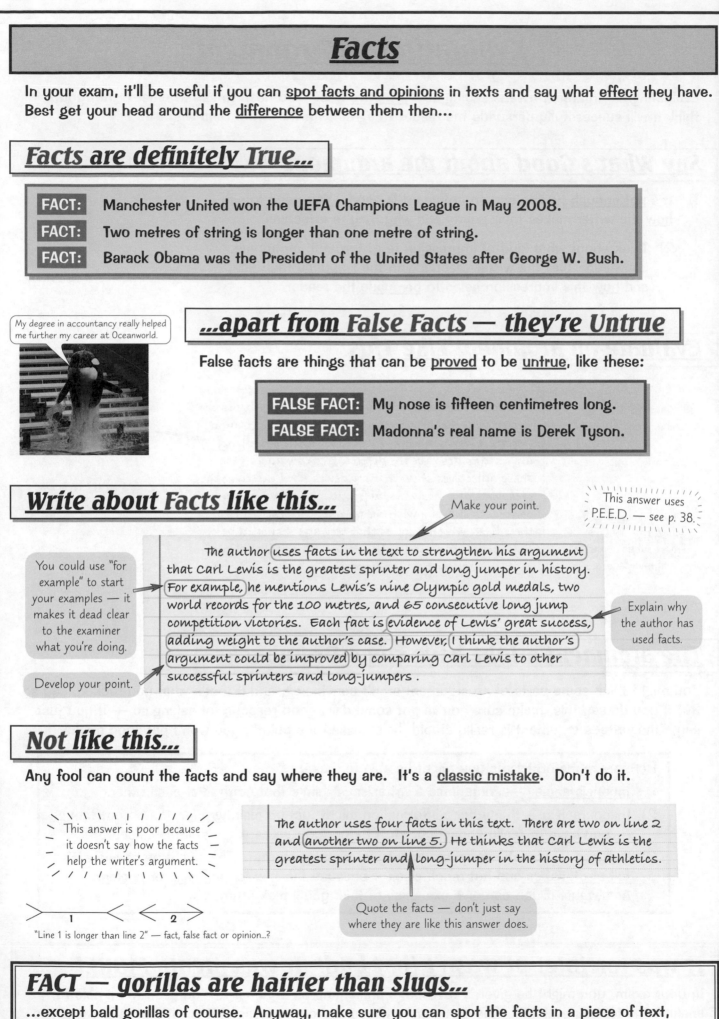

Opinions

Now you know a bit about facts, it's time for <u>opinions</u>.

Opinions aren't True or Untrue — they're just Beliefs

Different people can see the same thing in <u>different ways</u>. These are opinions, not facts — they're just what someone <u>thinks</u>. You <u>can't prove</u> that an opinion is true or untrue.

The words "I think" show that this is just a point of view.

OPINION: I think that animal testing for cosmetics should be banned.

OPINION: CD singles won't exist in ten years' time.

You can't prove this one way or the other yet.

Opinions can be given as <u>direct speech</u> (as if it's <u>spoken</u> by the <u>writer</u>), like in the two examples above. They can also be given as <u>reported dialogue</u> (spoken by <u>someone else</u>). This can make the opinions much more <u>convincing</u>.

EXAMPLE: A leading scientist says that animal testing for cosmetics should be banned.

This opinion is more convincing because it's what an expert thinks.

Some sentences contain both Opinions AND Facts

Sometimes you can get opinions and facts in the <u>same sentence</u>. Like this one:

FACT AND OPINION: Manchester United gloriously won the UEFA Champions League in May 2008.

The word "gloriously" is just an opinion...

...but the second bit is fact.

This kind of writing is often a <u>sign of bias</u>. Read more about bias on page 19.

Write about Opinions like this...

Mention all the effects the opinions have.

> The many opinions in this text (reinforce the author's points) and give the text an (informal tone.) The author uses satirical opinions to mock the target of her argument. For example: "Jamie Smith comes second in the contest for the World's most irritating display of chirpiness only to my three year old nephew at four o'clock on Christmas morning." The strength and humour of these opinions (create a powerful image) in the reader's mind, making the author's argument more persuasive. The light-hearted tone suggests that the (author's intention) is to make fun of Jamie Smith, rather than to seriously criticise him.

Remember to use P.E.E.D. — see p.38.

Explain why the author has used opinions.

Develop your point — e.g. comment on how the opinions reveal the author's attitude.

In my opinion, Hugh Jackman is extremely good-looking...

If a text presents different opinions, you might need to compare them. There are certain phrases that will help you to do this. Here's a few: similar to, contrasting with, on the other hand, different from, however, in agreement with, unlike, in the same way, conversely. All very useful.

Generalisations

Generalisations are sweeping statements that aren't necessarily true, like "young people today have no respect", or "Reality TV stars are all dim-witted, money-grabbing losers".

Generalisations make an argument more Forceful

1) A generalisation is a statement that's presented confidently as fact but doesn't give details.
2) Generalisations often make an argument sound more forceful and convincing, when it's actually not all that accurate.
3) They can be misleading — they often conveniently ignore facts that don't support them.
4) Generalisations sometimes create unfair stereotypes — e.g. "Foreign footballers are all cheats."

Generalisations look like this

Chips are bad for you.

Although it's true that eating loads of chips is unhealthy, most people reckon they're OK every now and again. Also, some types of chips are worse than others.

Smokers trying to quit usually have more success if they use nicotine patches.

There's no proof to back up this claim, but it sounds convincing.

Generalisations like this are often used in adverts, to try to give a positive impression of their product.

Write about generalisations Like This

In the exam, it'll be helpful if you can identify any generalisations and write about what effect they have.

This answer uses P.E.E.D. — see p.38.

Here's your point, made right at the start of your paragraph.

Here is your example.

The advertisement uses a generalisation when making claims about nicotine patches, when it says that "Smokers trying to quit usually have more success if they use nicotine patches." This is presented as a fact in order to convince the audience to buy the patches. However, I don't think it's a very effective advertisement, because no scientific evidence is given to back up the generalisation that's been used.

Here's your explanation.

This is where you develop your point.

Generalisation — an army promotion?

People use generalisations all the time. They're often used to exaggerate the truth, or to present a one-sided version of it, with carefully selected evidence that doesn't give the full story. If you can spot where a writer's used one, you can argue that their argument isn't as strong as it might seem.

Counter-arguments

Writers will often quote the <u>opposite point of view</u> first, then <u>argue against it</u>. This is a counter-argument — it strengthens the writer's own opinion by making it seem more reasonable.

Counter-arguments Disagree with the original argument

1) A counter-argument is when a writer presents one point of view, then <u>disagrees</u> with it, showing why it's wrong.

2) The counter-argument shows <u>why</u> the writer thinks another point of view is <u>wrong</u>. This makes the <u>writer's opinion</u> seem <u>better</u> in comparison.

3) Using a counter-argument shows that the writer has <u>considered other viewpoints</u>, instead of just jumping to an opinion. It makes them seem like a sensible, <u>thoughtful</u> person, instead of some ranting nutter.

Counter-arguments look like this

> Although many parents believe that eight hours' sleep is needed to learn effectively at school, studies show that the necessary amount actually varies greatly between different teenagers.

The first bit states an argument.

The second bit is the counter-argument — it picks holes in the original argument.

Write about counter-arguments Like This

First point out how the <u>original argument</u> and the <u>counter-argument</u> are made.

Show what the writer's counter-argument is.

> The writer presents the argument from the adult point of view when she says, "many parents believe that eight hours' sleep is needed to learn effectively", but then goes on to counter this argument by claiming that "the necessary amount actually varies greatly between different teenagers."

Show how the writer describes the original argument.

Then say <u>how</u> this technique strengthens the writer's argument — look at the <u>language</u> used.

Use quotes to show how the two sides of the argument come across differently.

> The word "believe" makes the parents' point of view sound unconvincing, as if there is no basis for it. The mention of "studies", on the other hand, makes the writer's own opinion sound well-informed. This makes the writer's point of view sound stronger and more valid than that of the parents.

Describe the effect of presenting the arguments in this way.

It doesn't mean disagreements between tables then...

Writers often present the opposite point of view as uninformed and irrational. They can then show their own opinion to be more sensible and well-researched. Another thing they can do is take specific things about the opposing point of view and one-by-one show that they're false.

Rhetoric

Rhetoric is when writers use <u>techniques</u> to make language more <u>persuasive</u> and <u>convincing</u>. The idea is to persuade their audience that there is only one sensible viewpoint — theirs.

Rhetorical Questions don't need an answer

1) Rhetorical questions are phrased to make the answer seem so <u>obvious</u> it's not even worth saying.

2) This makes the reader feel like they're <u>making their own mind up</u>, when actually the writer is deliberately trying to get them to think a <u>certain way</u>.

e.g. Can it really be fair to set students these ridiculous and unnecessary assignments?

The words "ridiculous" and "unnecessary" are put there to get the reader to think, "No, of course it's not fair."

Repetition emphasises key points

1) Writers <u>repeat</u> words or phrases to <u>emphasise</u> their most important points.

2) They're often repeated in <u>threes</u>.

e.g. It's outrageous to suggest that pupils don't work hard. It's outrageous to suggest that we should give up all our free time for study. Most of all though, it's outrageous to expect us to take on even more homework.

Write about rhetoric Like This

As always, make a <u>point</u>, give an <u>example</u>, explain the <u>effect</u> and <u>develop</u> your point.

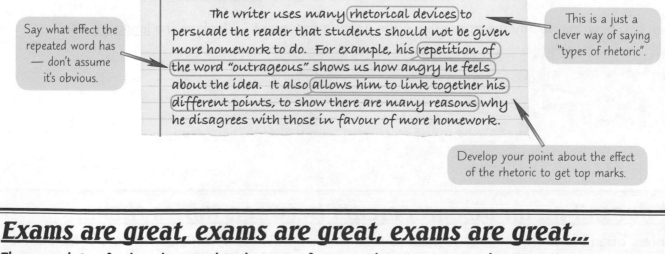

Say what effect the repeated word has — don't assume it's obvious.

The writer uses many (rhetorical devices) to persuade the reader that students should not be given more homework to do. For example, his (repetition of) the word "outrageous" shows us how angry he feels about the idea. It also (allows him to link together his) (different points, to show there are many reasons) why he disagrees with those in favour of more homework.

This is a just a clever way of saying "types of rhetoric".

Develop your point about the effect of the rhetoric to get top marks.

Exams are great, exams are great, exams are great...

There are lots of other <u>rhetorical techniques</u>, for example using emotive language (see page 34) or implications (suggesting something without saying it outright) to add to the text's impact.

Bias

If a text is biased, it <u>doesn't</u> give a <u>balanced</u> view. The writer's own point of view affects the writing, so it gives a misleading impression of the facts.

Biased Writing is affected by the writer's opinions

1) Biased writers don't usually lie, but they <u>don't give the full picture</u>.

2) Sometimes the writer <u>won't mention</u> something that opposes their argument, or they'll <u>exaggerate</u> something that supports it. Exaggerated language is also known as <u>hyperbole</u> (pronounced hi-PER-bow-lee — examiners just love it when you use fancy words).

3) Bias <u>isn't always obvious</u>, or even deliberate. Biased writers don't always make their opinion clear. They often <u>seem</u> to be talking in a neutral, factual way — while actually only presenting one point of view.

4) You need to be able to <u>recognise</u> bias, so that you don't mistake opinion for fact.

5) Biased writing often uses <u>generalisations</u> (see page 16).

Bias looks like this

> Coldplay are simply the best band to come out of this country since the Beatles. They have produced hit after hit on a regular basis, and perform to huge sell-out crowds. Their music is distinctive and yet subtle — it grabs you immediately and yet continues to offer new levels of creativity with every subsequent listen.

Jim Dodd and the Budgies — stiff competition.

1) The text above <u>ignores</u> the fact that lots of other bands have lots of hits and play to big audiences.

2) There's <u>no hard evidence</u> there — no facts and figures to back up the writer's claims.

3) The last sentence is just <u>opinion</u> — lots of people might completely <u>disagree</u> with this.

Write about bias Like This

Make a clear opening point.

Say if you think there's something missing from the writer's argument.

The writer is clearly biased in favour of Coldplay. He mentions "hit after hit" and "huge sell-out crowds", but does not give any details. There is no criticism and there are no comparisons with other bands to support the claim that they are the best "since the Beatles". This clear bias detracts from the writer's argument as he appears to have jumped to his opinion without finding any proper evidence for it.

Support it with short quotes.

Say what the overall effect of the bias is.

We're too expensive for you — you'll never bias...

A good way to spot bias is when the writer presents their opinion as fact, e.g. by saying something confidently but giving no evidence for it. This weakens their argument, as you can claim all sorts of absurd things this way — only yesterday someone tried to tell me that the moon's made of cheese.

Headlines

Presentational devices are used to make the page layout more interesting. You need to be able to say what specific <u>effects</u> they have. The beauty of them is that their effects are actually pretty obvious.

Headlines are there to grab your Attention

1) Headlines tell you, very briefly, <u>what</u> the article is <u>about</u>.

2) In newspapers and magazines, headlines are always <u>bigger</u> than all the other words, and are at the <u>top</u> of the page.

3) The point of headlines is to capture your <u>interest</u>, so you'll read the article.

4) Headlines sometimes use <u>humour</u>, <u>exaggeration</u> or <u>shocking facts</u> to grab your attention.

Headlines look like this

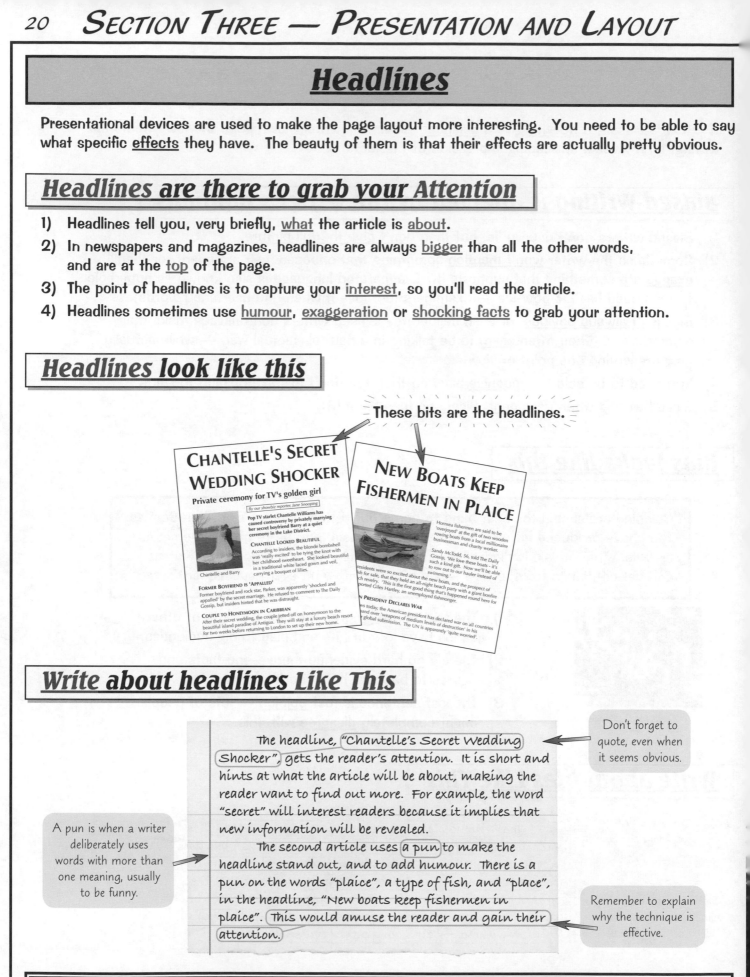

These bits are the headlines.

CHANTELLE'S SECRET WEDDING SHOCKER

Private ceremony for TV's golden girl

By our showbiz reporter, Jane Snooping

Pop TV starlet Chantelle Williams has caused controversy by privately marrying her secret boyfriend Barry at a quiet ceremony in the Lake District.

CHANTELLE LOOKED BEAUTIFUL

According to insiders, the blonde bombshell was 'really excited' to be tying the knot with her childhood sweetheart. She looked beautiful in a traditional white laced gown and veil, carrying a bouquet of lilies.

Chantelle and Barry

FORMER BOYFRIEND IS 'APPALLED'

Former boyfriend and rock star, Parker, was apparently 'shocked and appalled' by the secret marriage. He refused to comment to The Daily Gossip, but insiders hinted that he was distraught.

COUPLE TO HONEYMOON IN CARIBBEAN

After their secret wedding, the couple jetted off on honeymoon to the beautiful island paradise of Antigua. They will stay at a luxury beach resort for two weeks before returning to London to set up their new home.

NEW BOATS KEEP FISHERMEN IN PLAICE

Hornsea fishermen are said to be 'overjoyed' at the gift of two wooden rowing boats from a local millionaire businessman and charity worker.

Sandy McTodd, 56, told The Daily Gossip, 'We love these boats – it's such a kind gift. Now we'll be able to row out to our hauler instead of swimming.'

...residents were so excited about the new boats, and the prospect of ...sh for sale, that they held an all-night beach party with a giant bonfire ...ch revelry. 'This is the first good thing that's happened round here for ...ported Giles Hartley, an unemployed fishmonger.

...N PRESIDENT DECLARES WAR

...ws today, the American president has declared war on all countries ...sand over 'weapons of medium levels of destruction' in his ...r global submission. The UN is apparently 'quite worried'.

Write about headlines Like This

The headline, "Chantelle's Secret Wedding Shocker", gets the reader's attention. It is short and hints at what the article will be about, making the reader want to find out more. For example, the word "secret" will interest readers because it implies that new information will be revealed.

The second article uses a pun to make the headline stand out, and to add humour. There is a pun on the words "plaice", a type of fish, and "place", in the headline, "New boats keep fishermen in plaice". This would amuse the reader and gain their attention.

> Don't forget to quote, even when it seems obvious.

> A pun is when a writer deliberately uses words with more than one meaning, usually to be funny.

> Remember to explain why the technique is effective.

CGP Office Invaded by Dog in Pet Escape Scandal...

Headlines are there to attract your attention, so on some newspapers they're really big. If the headline's about something really exciting, it could be three inches tall — this makes it really stand out against its competitors on the newspaper stand when people are deciding which paper to buy.

Subheadings and Straplines

Subheadings and straplines are a bit like headlines, but, well, a bit different too. Read on.

Subheadings and Straplines help Organise the text

1) <u>Subheadings</u> are used to <u>split</u> the story up into little pieces to make it look less daunting and <u>easier to read</u>.

2) Each subheading briefly tells you <u>what</u> the next section of text is about.

3) They're usually a bit <u>bigger</u> than the rest of the text and might be <u>bold</u> or <u>underlined</u> to make them stand out.

1) <u>Straplines</u> are short statements that expand on what the headline says.

2) The text is <u>smaller</u> than the headline but <u>bigger</u> than the main text.

3) Straplines are found just <u>below</u> the headline.

4) The strapline tries to <u>hook</u> the reader, after the headline has got their initial interest.

Subheadings and Straplines look like this

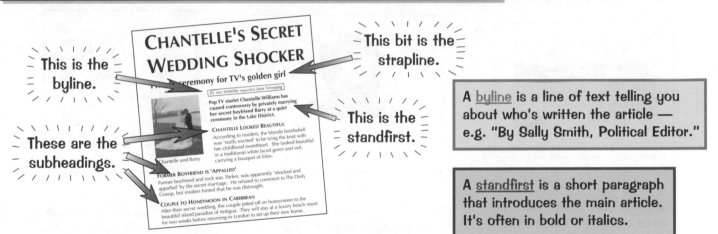

This is the byline.

These are the subheadings.

CHANTELLE'S SECRET WEDDING SHOCKER

...e ceremony for TV's golden girl

By our showbiz reporter, Jane Snooping

Pop TV starlet Chantelle Williams has caused controversy by privately marrying her secret boyfriend Barry at a quiet ceremony in the Lake District.

CHANTELLE LOOKED BEAUTIFUL
According to insiders, the blonde bombshell was 'really excited' to be tying the knot with her childhood sweetheart. She looked beautiful in a traditional white laced gown and veil, carrying a bouquet of lilies.

Chantelle and Barry

FORMER BOYFRIEND IS 'APPALLED'
Former boyfriend and rock star, Parker, was apparently 'shocked and appalled' by the secret marriage. He refused to comment to The Daily Gossip, but insiders hinted that he was distraught.

COUPLE TO HONEYMOON IN CARIBBEAN
After their secret wedding, the couple jetted off on honeymoon to the beautiful island paradise of Antigua. They will stay at a luxury beach resort for two weeks before returning to London to set up their new home.

This bit is the strapline.

This is the standfirst.

A <u>byline</u> is a line of text telling you about who's written the article — e.g. "By Sally Smith, Political Editor."

A <u>standfirst</u> is a short paragraph that introduces the main article. It's often in bold or italics.

Write about subheadings and straplines Like This

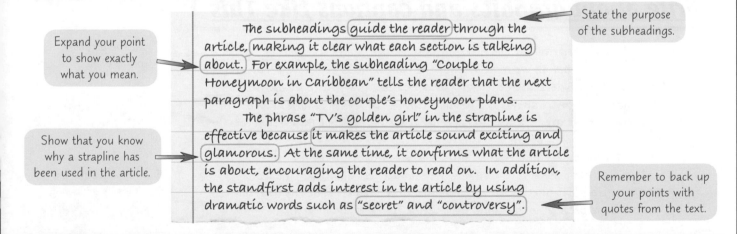

State the purpose of the subheadings.

Expand your point to show exactly what you mean.

Show that you know why a strapline has been used in the article.

Remember to back up your points with quotes from the text.

The subheadings guide the reader through the article, making it clear what each section is talking about. For example, the subheading "Couple to Honeymoon in Caribbean" tells the reader that the next paragraph is about the couple's honeymoon plans.

The phrase "TV's golden girl" in the strapline is effective because it makes the article sound exciting and glamorous. At the same time, it confirms what the article is about, encouraging the reader to read on. In addition, the standfirst adds interest in the article by using dramatic words such as "secret" and "controversy".

Subheadings — send in the substitute headteacher...

Remember — don't just say what the subheading or strapline is. Anyone can do that. Make sure, instead, that you write about the choice of words and most importantly, their effect on the reader. It's not hard, this stuff, but you'll lose marks if you don't give examples and explain your points.

Graphics and Captions

It's not only headlines and subheadings that make you want to start reading an article.
Photos and captions are also used to grab the reader's <u>attention</u> — this page shows you how.

Graphics and Captions give us lots of Information

1) Texts often have graphics, e.g. photos or diagrams, to <u>illustrate</u> what they're about.

2) They usually have <u>captions</u> with them — a short bit of text to explain what the graphic shows.

3) Sometimes graphics are used to emphasise a <u>feeling</u>. For example, photos of the effects of war make us see how <u>horrible</u> it must be.

4) Graphics can be specially <u>selected</u> or even <u>cropped</u> (cut or trimmed) to emphasise <u>one particular feeling</u> instead of others. E.g. a writer could make sure there are no <u>hopeful</u> photos of people being rescued in a war, that way we're <u>only shown</u> how horrible it is.

5) The reader can tell <u>what a text is about</u> just from a <u>quick glance</u> at the accompanying graphic.

Graphics and Captions look like this

Hurricane causes devastation

A lifetime of fun and affection — take me home

Friday, 9.00am

The photo shows more about the awful effects of the hurricane than the text alone could.

This picture is persuasive — the cute puppy is meant to make the reader feel a bit soppy.

The caption clarifies what's being shown — it tells you when the weather forecast is for.

Write about graphics and captions Like This

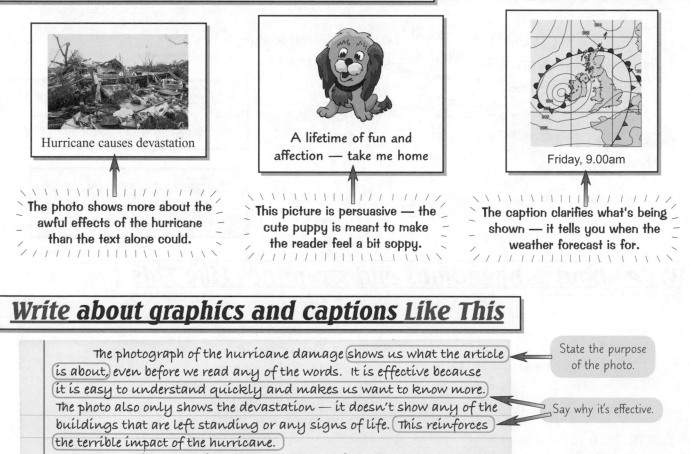

　　　The photograph of the hurricane damage (shows us what the article is about,) even before we read any of the words. It is effective because (it is easy to understand quickly and makes us want to know more.) The photo also only shows the devastation — it doesn't show any of the buildings that are left standing or any signs of life. (This reinforces the terrible impact of the hurricane.)
　　　The caption, "Hurricane causes devastation", tells us not only what happened, but also how we should feel about it. The word "devastation" in particular emphasises to the reader that the hurricane would have been a (horrendous experience for those involved.)

State the purpose of the photo.

Say why it's effective.

Show how effective the caption is by describing its effect on the reader.

Smile — it could be worse...

Remember, the graphic always goes with the words in the article and is effective because it shows us what the article is about. Don't just say what the graphic is, say why it's effective and how it connects to the rest of the text too. And remember to describe the emotional impact it has.

Text Columns

Now you know how writers can grab your attention, you need to be able to talk about how they keep you interested. Text columns are one of their little ploys.

Text can be Broken Up into Columns

1) Writers don't want you to get <u>bored</u> or <u>confused</u>, so they often break their text up into columns — it makes it appear shorter and <u>easier to read</u>.

2) Columns can also make certain bits of text <u>easier to find</u>.

3) You see <u>text columns</u> all over the place — in magazines, newspapers, adverts etc.

Columns look like this

1) Here's an example that you might see in a cinema advert. Different bits of text are found in different columns, which makes information <u>easier to find</u>.

Percy Jackson and the Lightning Thief	PG	19:00, 21:00, 22:00
The Princess and the Frog	U	14:20, 15:40, 18:00
Avatar	12A	15:00, 16:40, 20:00

This column tells you the name of the film.

This column tells you the film's certificate.

This column tells you when the film is on.

2) Here's an example that you might see in a newspaper or magazine.

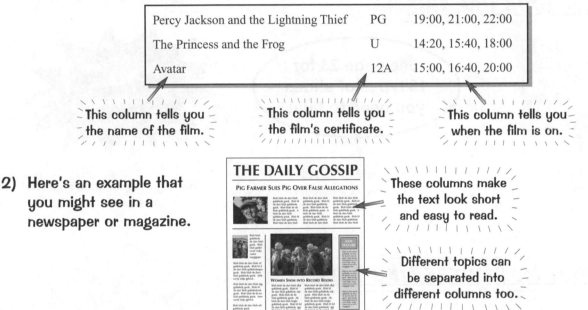

THE DAILY GOSSIP

PIG FARMER SUES PIG OVER FALSE ALLEGATIONS

WOMEN SWIM INTO RECORD BOOKS

These columns make the text look short and easy to read.

Different topics can be separated into different columns too.

Write about text columns Like This

In the first example, the author has divided the information into three columns. He has done this to show the different types of information clearly. The effect of this is that everyone can find the information they need quickly without having to read everything. For example, someone looking for a film suitable for a child under 12 would see the "U" in the second column and not need to read the other lines. This makes the information really clear.

However, in the second example, text columns have been used differently. Here, the writer uses text columns to make the text appear shorter and easier to read. Text columns like these break up the text, so readers aren't put off by large blocks of text.

Show you know how these text columns work.

This word shows the examiner that you are making a comparison.

Text columns — ooh, how exciting...

If you don't really get it, just think about a newspaper without the columns. Imagine that all the writing just went from left to right in a giant block across the page. It'd be daunting to read — people would be scared away by the amount of text. Columns are a clever little trick really.

Text Boxes

Text boxes are used to make important information <u>stand out</u>, or just to break up the text.

Text can be put into Boxes

1) Text boxes are used to make certain important parts of the text <u>stand out</u> in order to grab your <u>attention</u>. This may make you more <u>interested</u> in reading an article or even help persuade you to <u>buy</u> a newspaper or magazine.

2) Different bits of text can be put in separate <u>boxes</u> in order to <u>break up</u> the main text and make it appear easier to read.

3) Sometimes the text can be at an <u>angle</u>, to make it <u>stand out</u> more.

Jeremy always keeps his text boxes nice and tidy.

Text Boxes look like this

12 year old boy who saved brother, says "I wish I'd never helped him".

This might be found in a newspaper or magazine article. It highlights a bit of the story.

See page 23 for 15 types of shoes you need to buy!

This might be found on the cover of a magazine. It will get people interested.

Order your free DVD now — online, by phone or by mail.

This might be found in an advert. It gives you instructions.

Write about text boxes Like This

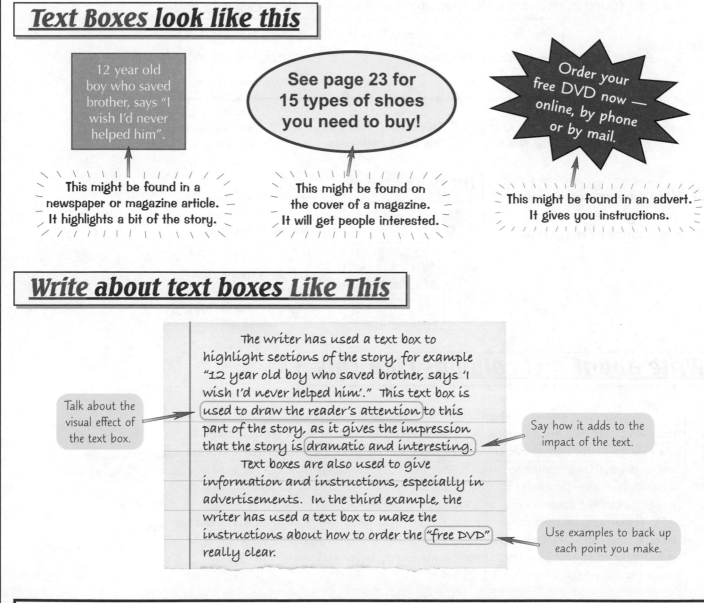

The writer has used a text box to highlight sections of the story, for example "12 year old boy who saved brother, says 'I wish I'd never helped him'." This text box is used to draw the reader's attention to this part of the story, as it gives the impression that the story is dramatic and interesting.

Text boxes are also used to give information and instructions, especially in advertisements. In the third example, the writer has used a text box to make the instructions about how to order the "free DVD" really clear.

Talk about the visual effect of the text box.

Say how it adds to the impact of the text.

Use examples to back up each point you make.

Bruno and Tyson compete via mobile phone...

I bet you don't believe how important this stuff is... Well just go to your local newsagents and have a look at all the magazines and newspapers on display. Every single cover staring back at you will show a number of exciting text boxes, all enticing you to read their articles and get their free gifts.

SECTION THREE — PRESENTATION AND LAYOUT

Bullet Points and Numbered Lists

Now that you understand how text boxes and text columns work, it's time to look at other devices that writers use to make sure their work is clearly presented and easy to understand.

Bullet Points and Numbered Lists break texts down

1) <u>Bullet points</u> are <u>dots</u>, <u>dashes</u> or other <u>symbols</u> that go at the start of each new point in a <u>list</u>.

2) Sometimes lists can be <u>numbered</u> instead.

3) Bullet points and numbered lists are often used when writers want to give you <u>lots of information</u>. They separate complex information into <u>step-by-step</u> points, to make it <u>easier to read</u>.

Bullet Points and Numbered Lists look like this

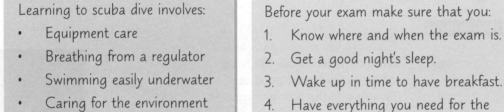

Learning to scuba dive involves:

• Equipment care
• Breathing from a regulator
• Swimming easily underwater
• Caring for the environment
• Being safe

Dots are used as bullet points.

These points give you information.

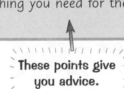

Before your exam make sure that you:

1. Know where and when the exam is.
2. Get a good night's sleep.
3. Wake up in time to have breakfast.
4. Have everything you need for the exam.

This is a numbered list.

These points give you advice.

I'm sure there was something I had to do today...

Tracy had forgotten point 5 — do the exam.

Write about bullet points and numbered lists Like This

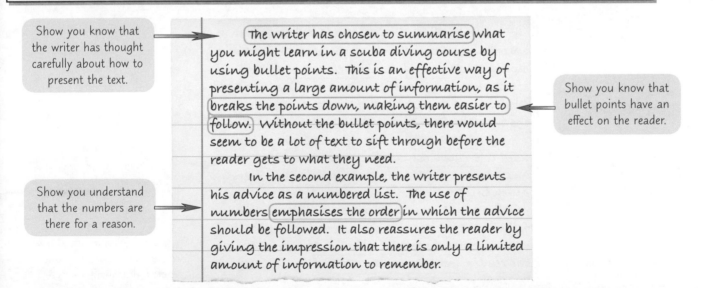

Show you know that the writer has thought carefully about how to present the text.

Show you understand that the numbers are there for a reason.

The writer has chosen to summarise what you might learn in a scuba diving course by using bullet points. This is an effective way of presenting a large amount of information, as it breaks the points down, making them easier to follow. Without the bullet points, there would seem to be a lot of text to sift through before the reader gets to what they need.

In the second example, the writer presents his advice as a numbered list. The use of numbers emphasises the order in which the advice should be followed. It also reassures the reader by giving the impression that there is only a limited amount of information to remember.

Show you know that bullet points have an effect on the reader.

My bullet points didn't work — they must've been blanks...

OK, it doesn't take a genius to spot a bullet point, but it's still worth writing about them. Show the examiner that you understand the effect different ways of presenting text can have on the reader, and you can get yourself a couple of extra marks — which is always nice.

Colour

"Wow, look at all the colours!" said Bob Grey the boredom inspector. "Grey, brown, beige... cream! It's all too exciting. I think I need a lie down."

Colour affects how you Read a text

1) <u>Colours</u> can affect how we read a text — e.g. the colour of the <u>text</u> and the <u>background</u>.

2) Writers and the people who publish media texts know this, which means that when they use colours, they're using them on purpose for a particular <u>effect</u>.

3) For example, lots of <u>bright colours</u> could suggest that an article is about a <u>fun</u> topic, like dancing, while <u>dark colours</u> might be used to create a <u>serious</u> mood for an article about war.

Colour is Used like this

Real-life stories

Blah blah de darr blah dhjt gobbledy gook. Blah basl de darr blah gobbledy xdfdgy gook. Blah blah de b blah gobbledy gook. Ab blah blah de darr blah fergki bloh gobbledy gook. Blah bl frd de darr blah gobbledy tgjj Blah blah de darr

De darr blah fergki bloh gobbledy gook. Blah bl frd de darr blah gobbledy tgjj Blah blah de darr blah erx

This is no ordinary tiger — it's my new husband!

frljn lah blah de darr blah dh sgge gobbledy gook. Blah ba de darr blah gobbledy xdfdgy gook. Blah blah de da dad d 'ah gobbledy gook darr l

frljn lah blah de darr blah dh sgge gobbledy gook. Blah ba de darr blah gobbledy xdfdgy 'lah blah.

frljn lah blah de darr blah dj sgge gobbledy gook. Blah sl gobbledy xdfdgy 'rd a

This page has an orange colour scheme. It reinforces the topic of tigers, and looks good as a whole with the tiger picture.

Heavenly Food
• Fruit
• Vegetables
• Nuts
• Whole grain cereal

Sinful Food
• Chocolate
• Crisps
• Chips
• Deep fried f

Different-coloured backgrounds are used to create a contrast between "heavenly" and "sinful" foods.

Write about colour Like This

Show that you understand the effect of colour on the reader.

In the first text, the page has been given an orange colour scheme. Orange is a bright and exciting colour, and its use creates a dramatic effect, (drawing the reader's attention) to the page. Orange is also the colour of tigers, so it adds to the tiger theme.

In the second example, colours have been used to (create a contrast) between "heavenly" and "sinful" foods. The heavenly side has been given bright, light, pure-looking colours, which reinforce the heavenly theme and make the reader feel relaxed. The sinful side is red and black, which creates a sense of evil and danger, making the reader (feel tense and uneasy).

Show that you understand how colour can be used to exaggerate differences.

Show that you understand how colour can be used to make people feel different emotions.

Sadly there isn't a "colouring in" part of the exam...

Sometimes colour is used to draw your attention to something, but often it has more meaning. Traditionally, we associate red with danger, bright colours with excitement, and dull colours with boring or serious things. Also look out for contrasting colours which often emphasise a difference.

Font Styles

You need to remember that everything on a page tells you something about the text.
This includes what the writing looks like and which font it is written in.

Fonts are different Styles of printed text

1) The <u>font</u> of a text gives you a clue about <u>what kind</u> of text it is.
2) Serious, formal fonts are for <u>serious</u>, formal texts.
3) Cartoony, childish fonts are for <u>light-hearted</u> texts, or texts for <u>children</u>.
4) Some fonts look like <u>handwriting</u> and some can even look <u>spooky</u> or <u>romantic</u> for example.

The mischievous smile meant she'd written her speech in Litterbox ICG again.

Here are some examples of Different Fonts

> There will be a community watch meeting at the village hall on Sunday.

Look how formal and serious this font is.

> There will be a brownie/scout meeting at the village hall on Sunday.

This font is clear and easy to read, without being too official-looking.

> There will be a drama club meeting at the village hall on Sunday.

This font is harder to read, but looks impressive and arty.

> **Serif** fonts have little lines or curly bits on the ends of the letters, like this. They usually look quite formal.
>
> **Sans serif** fonts are simpler and don't have extra bits, like this.

Write about font style Like This

State what kind of audience the font will appeal to.

You don't need to know the names of the fonts — just describe them.

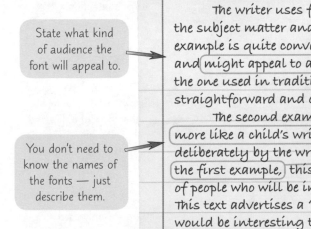

The writer uses font styles that are appropriate for the subject matter and audience. The font in the first example is quite conventional. It is easy to read, formal and might appeal to an older audience. This font is like the one used in traditional newspapers because it is so straightforward and clear.

The second example is written in a font that looks more like a child's writing and has been chosen deliberately by the writer to appeal to children. Just as in the first example, this font is meant to attract the kind of people who will be interested in what the text is about. This text advertises a "brownie/scout meeting" which would be interesting to children.

Show that you can see the similarities and differences between texts.

The best font is ZapfDingbats — ✻▼ ▲✻✽◆❄✳✽ ■✻☐✗...

Remember, the font tells you about the tone of the text at first glance. So a serious, boring font tells you that the text is probably very formal and is not a laughing matter. A silly, cartoony font tells you that the text is light-hearted, jokey and informal. It's not rocket science, this font stuff.

Font Formatting

Formatting means making words or sentences stand out from the rest of the text, for example by making them **bold** or *italic*, underlining them or putting them in CAPITALS.

Fonts can be Formatted to create different Effects

1) The way a font is formatted is just as important as the type of font used.

2) Different styles of the same font have different effects on the reader.

3) Writers format fonts to emphasise particular words or phrases and make them really stand out. To do this, they make them look different from the rest of the text.

Formatting looks like this

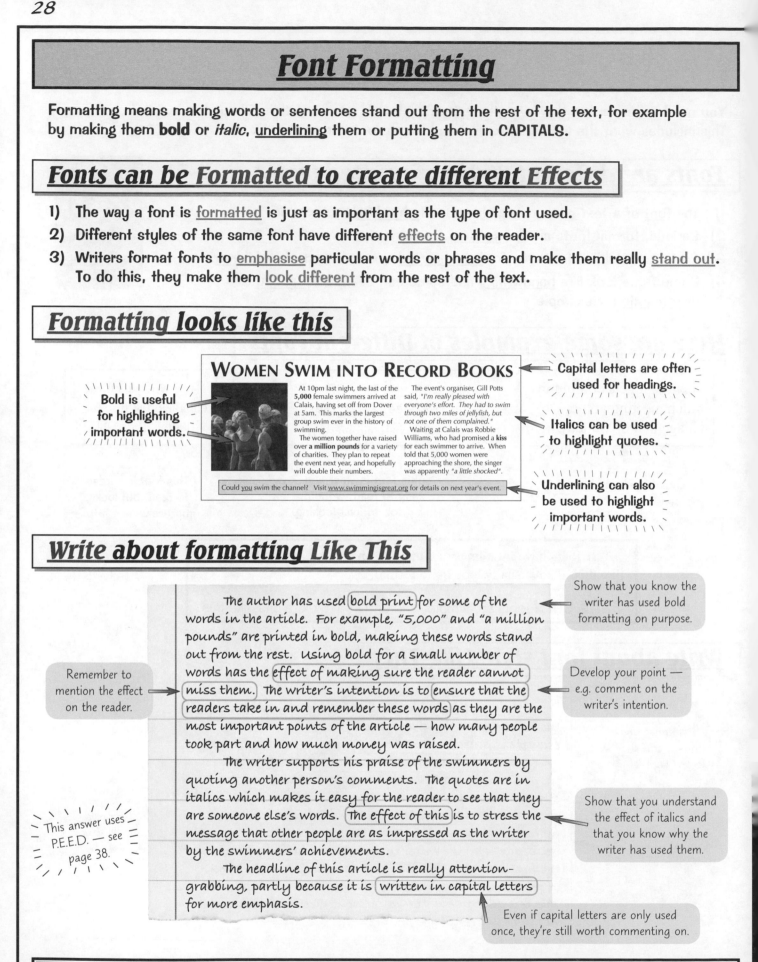

WOMEN SWIM INTO RECORD BOOKS

At 10pm last night, the last of the **5,000** female swimmers arrived at Calais, having set off from Dover at 5am. This marks the largest group swim ever in the history of swimming.

The women together have raised over **a million pounds** for a variety of charities. They plan to repeat the event next year, and hopefully will double their numbers.

The event's organiser, Gill Potts said, *"I'm really pleased with everyone's effort. They had to swim through two miles of jellyfish, but not one of them complained."*

Waiting at Calais was Robbie Williams, who had promised a **kiss** for each swimmer to arrive. When told that 5,000 women were approaching the shore, the singer was apparently *"a little shocked"*.

Could you swim the channel? Visit www.swimmingisgreat.org for details on next year's event.

Bold is useful for highlighting important words.

Capital letters are often used for headings.

Italics can be used to highlight quotes.

Underlining can also be used to highlight important words.

Write about formatting Like This

The author has used bold print for some of the words in the article. For example, "5,000" and "a million pounds" are printed in bold, making these words stand out from the rest. Using bold for a small number of words has the effect of making sure the reader cannot miss them. The writer's intention is to ensure that the readers take in and remember these words as they are the most important points of the article — how many people took part and how much money was raised.

The writer supports his praise of the swimmers by quoting another person's comments. The quotes are in italics which makes it easy for the reader to see that they are someone else's words. The effect of this is to stress the message that other people are as impressed as the writer by the swimmers' achievements.

The headline of this article is really attention-grabbing, partly because it is written in capital letters for more emphasis.

Show that you know the writer has used bold formatting on purpose.

Remember to mention the effect on the reader.

Develop your point — e.g. comment on the writer's intention.

This answer uses P.E.E.D. — see page 38.

Show that you understand the effect of italics and that you know why the writer has used them.

Even if capital letters are only used once, they're still worth commenting on.

I'd like to do some formatting, if I may be so bold...

When you are comparing how pieces of text are presented, write about the differences and similarities in the font style and formatting. But make sure you remember to write about the effects that these different styles of font have on the readers too. That's the only way to get decent marks.

Descriptive Language

The texts you have to write about in the exam will use lots of different language techniques to make them more effective. You need to be able to recognise the techniques and say why they're used.

Descriptive Language makes text Interesting

1) Writers use descriptive techniques so that the reader gets a really clear <u>image</u> in their head of what the writer's describing. It makes the text more <u>interesting</u>, <u>dramatic</u> and <u>real</u>.

2) <u>Descriptive language</u> includes <u>imagery</u> such as metaphors, similes and personification. (See pages 30-31 for more on these.)

3) Writers often give <u>descriptions</u> based on their five <u>senses</u> (what they can <u>see</u>, <u>smell</u>, <u>hear</u>, <u>touch</u> or <u>taste</u>).

4) Another sign of descriptive language is when the writer uses lots of <u>adjectives</u> — describing words like "huge" or "fiery" that give a specific <u>impression</u> of something. This technique is known as <u>story-telling style</u>.

Rex could think of plenty of words to describe what he'd just heard.

> **EXAMPLE** After the dreary, grey sheet of rain had swept over the land, the parched, sun-baked fields transformed into a fertile, emerald-green valley.

5) Writers can also <u>build up</u> the description of something <u>throughout</u> their work. For example, they might do this by writing sentences with <u>contrasting</u> descriptions or descriptions that <u>agree</u> with each other. That way, <u>more detail</u> is added to the description as you read each sentence.

6) The way a piece of writing is <u>structured</u> can also help to develop description. Lots of <u>simple</u>, <u>short</u> sentences create a <u>fast-paced</u>, <u>exciting</u> description. <u>Longer</u>, more <u>complicated</u> sentences mean descriptions are built up <u>slowly</u>, more <u>gently</u> and with <u>lots of detail</u>.

Write about descriptive language Like This

The writer uses descriptive language to show the effect of the rain on the African landscape. In the first part of the sentence he uses adjectives such as "dreary" and "grey" to describe the rain. This creates a downbeat, unhappy image. He reinforces this impression by going on to describe the land as being "parched" and the fields "sun-baked". The writer then contrasts these images with the "fertile, emerald-green valley" that has been created. This allows the reader to picture in his or her own mind just how dramatic the changes that the rains bring are. Perhaps the writer is trying to show, through the contrast of negative images with positive images, that the time after the rains are a time of great joy.

This answer uses P.E.E.D.

Here are your <u>examples</u>

Describe any <u>techniques</u> that the writer has used to build up the description.

<u>Explain</u> why the writer has used descriptive language.

<u>Develop</u> your point, e.g. say what you think the writer's <u>intention</u> is.

To get the marks, you need to <u>examine</u> the use of descriptive language — say <u>why</u> you think it makes the text more interesting for the reader.

My dad used descriptive language when I broke his mug...

It's not too hard to get the hang of writing about these techniques — just spot where one's been used, quote it, and explain how it's been used deliberately to affect the reader in some way. Easy.

Metaphors and Similes

Metaphors and similes are both types of <u>imagery</u>. They're different ways of <u>comparing</u> things.

Metaphors and similes are Comparisons

Metaphors and similes describe one thing by <u>comparing</u> it to something else. Writers use them to create a <u>picture</u> in the <u>reader's mind</u>.

> **Metaphors** describe something by saying that it <u>is</u> something else.

EXAMPLE Suddenly we were in the middle of the war zone. I tried to run but my feet <u>were</u> blocks of concrete.

> **Similes** describe something by saying that it's <u>like</u> something else. They usually use the words <u>as</u> or <u>like</u>.

EXAMPLE Sitting on my balcony, the humid Italian air clings to my skin <u>like</u> a warm, wet blanket.

Write about metaphors Like This

This answer uses P.E.E.D.

Here's your point, made right at the start of your paragraph.

Here's your explanation.

The journalist uses a metaphor when reporting from the war zone, "I tried to run but my feet were blocks of concrete". This direct comparison gives the reader a sense of the reporter's panic at being in such a frightening situation that, try as he might, he was too scared to flee. I think the use of this metaphor makes the description really effective because it helps the readers to empathise with the journalist.

Here's your example.

Here's where you develop your point.

Write about similes Like This

This quote is tucked neatly into the sentence. Examiners love embedded quotations like this.

The writer uses a simile when describing the humid weather in Italy. By comparing the air to a "warm, wet blanket", the reader can really feel just how unpleasantly damp and sticky the air is.

Don't do it like this

This is too general. Write about <u>one</u> of the metaphors or similes in particular.

The writer uses lots of metaphors and similes which make it more interesting.

Don't just say it makes it more interesting. To get the marks, you need to say <u>why</u> it makes the text more interesting for the reader.

The spectre of the exam lurked like an invisible tiger...

Metaphors — his breath was ice, my boss is a pussycat really, your trainers are pure cheese.
Similes — his breath was as cold as ice, my boss is as nice as a cat, your trainers smell like cheese.

Analogy and Personification

Analogy, personification — too many new words? Sorry about that...

Analogies are just fancy Comparisons

An <u>analogy</u> is a kind of extended <u>simile</u> (see page 30 for more on similes).
The writer simply <u>compares</u> two different things to explain what they're saying and make it clearer.

> **EXAMPLES**
>
> Hoping your exams will go OK without opening your books is like hoping for a win on the lottery without ever having bought a ticket.
>
> Deforestation is happening at an incredible speed. An area of rainforest equal to twenty football pitches is lost every minute.

Write about analogies Like This

Here's your example.

Try to make your point in the first sentence.

Develop your point — say why the writer wants to affect the reader in this way.

Explain the effect of the analogy on the reader.

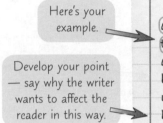

To help him explain about deforestation, the writer uses an analogy when he says that, "An area of rainforest equal to twenty football pitches is lost every minute." This allows the audience to understand the phenomenal speed of this destruction, by making a comparison which they can easily visualise. The use of this analogy increases the impact that the information has on the reader, making the writer's argument more persuasive.

Personification is describing a thing as a Person

1) Personification means describing something <u>as if it's a person</u>, or sometimes an <u>animal</u> — in the way it looks, moves, sounds or some other aspect of it.

2) Personification makes descriptions seem to "<u>come to life</u>".

3) It can also help to give a sense of how the <u>writer feels</u> about something.

> **EXAMPLE** Military helicopters prowl the city, their menacing mechanical voices threatening to stamp out any sign of activity.

Write about personification Like This

Say what impression the personification creates.

As always, give examples.

Develop your idea.

The writer's use of personification makes the helicopters appear threatening and dangerous. She describes how they "prowl the city", making it appear to be the helicopters themselves who are in charge, rather than the people controlling them. The "menacing mechanical voices" add to the impression of a frightening, evil force controlling the city. The writer is implying that the military helicopters are not a positive presence. I think she strongly disapproves of the military presence in the city.

I hate comparing — I've got analogy to it...

Have you noticed how both these answers use point, example, explain, develop (P.E.E.D.)? Funny that, perhaps there's something in it... Don't make your point too long though — you've got room to explain and develop it later. And quote something, even if it's hard to choose a good example.

Alliteration and Onomatopoeia

Writers use lots of different techniques to stop their readers getting bored.
Alliteration and onomatopoeia are used as sound effects in writing to keep readers interested.

Alliteration means repeating the same Sound

Alliteration is when words that are close together begin with the same sound. It makes
the sentence seem more interesting to the reader. Alliteration is often found in headlines:

P.M.'s Panic   Rooney Rules the Roost   Close Call for Kids   Magic Murray Marches on

In the exam you'll need to be able to identify alliteration and write about how and why it's been used.

Write about alliteration Like This

Here's your point, right in the first sentence.

Here's an example.

By using the alliteration of "Magic Murray Marches on", the newspaper attracts the reader's attention to the article on Andy Murray at Wimbledon. Alliteration emphasises the headline and gives the article a snappy, easy-to-read opening which encourages readers to continue.

Explain why the writer has used alliteration...

...and develop your point.

Onomatopoeia means words that Imitate Noises

Onomatopoeia means words that sound like the noises being described. This makes the
description of the sounds more vivid to the reader. Here are some good examples:

Thud   Slurp   Crackle   Smash   Tinkle   Screech   Hiss   Squish

Write about onomatopoeia Like This

Remember the effect on the reader.

Here's the example.

Including the onomatopoeic word "slurp" in the cartoon used in the milkshake advertisement makes the audience recognise the humorous noise often made by children when they drink. As the advert is aimed at children, this helps them to identify with the cartoon character and therefore make the product being advertised appeal to them.

Think about the purpose of the text when you're writing about onomatopoeia.

Onomatopoeia — what a stupid word...

Learn how to spell ON-O-MAT-O-POEI-A. You'll impress the examiner if you can spell it correctly.
It's hard, I know, but just write it out a few times and you'll get the hang of it eventually.

Irony and Sarcasm

Irony and sarcasm are techniques that are related to the <u>tone</u> of the writing (see glossary).

Irony *is saying the* Opposite *of what you* Mean

1) <u>Irony</u> is when the <u>literal meaning</u> of a piece of writing is the exact <u>opposite</u> of its <u>intended meaning</u>.

2) The reader can tell the writer is being ironic from the context of the writing.

3) Irony is often <u>humorous</u> or <u>light-hearted</u>.

EXAMPLE We were stranded at the airport for 48 hours with no food, which was just great.

Of course, the writer doesn't <u>really</u> mean it was great. In fact, he means it was the <u>opposite</u> of great.

Write *about irony* Like This

Here's your point. Say <u>why</u> the writer has used irony.

Here's your evidence.

The writer uses irony to express his frustration at having his flight delayed for two days. When he says that being there for 48 hours with no food was "just great" he actually means the opposite — that the lack of food added to his annoyance and irritation. He is using irony to amuse the reader, whilst also making them feel sympathetic towards him.

Don't forget to use P.E.E.D...

Here's your explanation.

Here's where you develop your point.

Sarcasm *is* Nastier *than irony*

1) The word "<u>sarcasm</u>" comes from a Greek word that literally means "<u>flesh tearing</u>".

2) <u>Sarcasm</u> is language that has a <u>mocking</u> or <u>scornful</u> tone. It's often intended to <u>insult someone</u> or <u>make fun</u> of them, or to show that the writer is <u>angry</u> or <u>annoyed</u> about something.

3) Sarcastic writing often uses <u>irony</u> — but the tone is more <u>aggressive</u> and <u>unpleasant</u>.

EXAMPLE The council's latest brainwave on tackling petty crime is to take away the few local facilities available to youngsters. This is presumably intended to encourage them to stay indoors watching Hollyoaks rather than engaging with society in any way.

Write *about sarcasm* Like This

The writer's use of sarcasm in describing the council's "brainwave" shows how stupid he thinks the scheme is. His sarcastic comment that it is "presumably intended" to exclude young people from society suggests that the council have not thought it through. Rather than being a clever way of reducing crime, he clearly believes it will make the problem worse.

Show the intended effect of the sarcasm.

Say what the writer is implying, and how it adds to their argument.

Sarcasm, yeah right, what a great technique...

One kind of text that often uses irony and sarcasm is <u>satire</u>. Satire is designed to make fun out of a particular person or thing. They're often political, with the intention of ruining the reputation of a politician or government by imitating them but emphasising their bad points.

Technical and Emotive Language

Some of the texts in the exam might use technical language to sound knowledgeable and add detail. Others may use more emotive language to try to persuade you to take their point of view.

Technical language is often used to Support an argument

1) Technical language includes things like specialist terms, jargon and statistics. It gives an impression of the writer having in-depth knowledge of the topic they're writing about.

2) You'll find technical language in textbooks, instructions, reports, and even newspaper articles.

3) It's often used to present facts to support an argument, making it more convincing to the reader.

> **EXAMPLE** Governments need to act now to combat climate change. Average worldwide temperatures have increased by about 1°C in the last hundred years, mainly due to increased emission of greenhouse gases such as carbon dioxide and methane.

Write about technical language Like This

Describe the impression the technical details create.

By including technical terms relating to climate change, such as "Average worldwide temperatures" and "greenhouse gases", the writer gives the impression that he understands the finer details of the issue. This implication supports his argument that governments need to take more action to deal with climate change.

Say how it helps the writer's argument.

Emotive language is used to Persuade

1) Writers use emotive language to get the reader to feel really strongly about something. This could be feelings of disgust, sadness, happiness, anger or any other emotion.

2) Language is often made emotive by strong adjectives, e.g. "shocking", "shameful" or "heroic".

3) Emotive language can emphasise a point — it usually makes the writer's opinion very clear.

> **EXAMPLE** The bears are forced to perform these painful dances and are frequently subjected to physical abuse.

Write about emotive language Like This

Say how the emotive language is used.

The leaflet against animal cruelty uses highly emotive language. The words "forced" and "painful" are used to manipulate the reader's response, persuading them to feel, as the writer does, that this treatment is inhumane and unjustifiable.

Talk about the overall effect on the reader.

Here comes the science...

Two more types of language to learn here, but nothing too hard to get your head around. Technical language can be used to give detail, but more often than not it's there to make the author sound like they know what they're on about. And emotive language makes you emotional. Tricky eh?

Tabloid Newspaper Language

Tabloid newspapers use quite a distinctive style of writing. There are masses of different features you'll be able to talk about in your exam if you get a tabloid newspaper article.

Tabloids use a Specific Style of language

Tabloid newspapers, e.g. The Sun and The News of the World, are small, almost square-shaped and usually have big headlines, photos and opinionated articles. Here are some examples of tabloid newspaper style, or "tabloidese" as it's sometimes called:

Nicknames are used to make the reader think about the person being written about as someone they know well. It gives them a sense of familiarity. They're most often used for celebrities.

> Examples include: "Fergie", "Posh and Becks", "Princess Di".

Slang words, colloquialisms (conversational language), informal language and short, simple sentences are used to make the readers feel that the newspaper is chatting to them, as if they're someone they know and trust.

> Examples include: "soap stars in spat", "we won a whopping £30 million", "celebs".

Puns and wordplay are used to make the newspaper seem jokey and fun.

> Examples include: "Sven's he going?", "Brad's the Pitts".

Tabloid Style looks like this

FRANKIE FANS THE FLAMES

By our sports writer, Rick Roberts

Hopping-mad Wabbingford City manager Sid Franklin has lashed out at star-striker turncoat Ruud Van der Livary after his Wednesday walkout.

Fed up Frankie blasted the one-time darling of Dale Road after he turned down a new contract at Wabbingford for a megabucks deal at French side FC Montjoi.

Ruud awakening

"Obviously our offer wasn't good enough so he ran off to his luxury yacht", Frankie fumed. "Then I got a message from his agent saying the deal's dead in the water.

"I'm gutted but I'll accept it because I only want players who are committed, not greedy money-grabbers."

The bust-up started when Rowdy Ruud's agent, Theo Gimidosch, accused Wabbingford of "dithering" over a suggested new contract.

Write about tabloid journalism Like This

The headline of this tabloid article is designed to instantly attract the reader's interest. The alliteration of "Frankie Fans the Flames" grabs the reader's attention. The use of the nickname "Frankie" suggests that the article has inside information, as it gives the impression that the writer knows the person involved.

Puns and slang expressions are used throughout the article. For example, "Ruud awakening" has a play on words with the player's name and the word "rude". This creates a light-hearted tone and keeps the reader amused enough to read the full article.

> Use the right terms.

> Say why the newspaper has used this technique.

> Keep referring closely to the text.

I just can't stand all those puns that tabloids use...

I bet you thought that GCSE English would be all Shakespeare and poetry. Nope, you get to read all the latest hot gossip about badly behaved footballers and celebrity romances too. Lucky you.

Structure

"Structure" means the way different parts of a text are put together. These examples are all from newspaper articles, but the same trends tend to occur in other non-fiction texts.

Introductions create Interest in the text

1)   An introduction should <u>briefly</u> give the reader the <u>main points</u> of the article.
2)   It should also <u>interest</u> the reader enough to read the <u>rest</u> of the article.

e.g. Fears were voiced last night for the safety of the lone whale who was spotted in the Thames by the Embankment in Central London. Onlookers have nicknamed him "Willy" and have taken to the banks of the river to watch. Marine biologists are on hand to oversee the task of returning "Willy" to the wild.

Unusual information and emotive words make the reader want to find out more.

Gives the reader the main points.

Write about introductions Like This

Make your point straight away.

The introduction of this text is effective because of the tone and the language used. The emotive words in the first sentence, such as "Fears", "safety" and "lone", immediately interest the reader. In addition, the introduction gives the main points of the article so that the reader can understand what it is about as well as deciding whether to read on.

Here are some good examples.

Show that you understand the key purposes of the introduction.

The middle tells you Who, What, Where, When and Why

After the introduction, the main bit of text gives the <u>answers</u> to all the questions that readers might want to ask — <u>who</u>, <u>what</u>, <u>where</u>, <u>when</u> and <u>why</u>.

e.g.

Tells us <u>who</u> it's about.

Tells us <u>when</u> it's happening.

Tells us <u>what</u> is going on.

David Blaine, the enigmatic American illusionist, who first found fame when he was spotted performing his card tricks on the streets of New York, has chosen his home city to attempt to outdo any of his contemporaries. He will spend the next week in a giant goldfish bowl in order to try to break a world record for the longest time under water.

Nathan and his team were trying to figure out who, what, where, when and why.

Tells us <u>where</u> it's happening.

Tells us <u>why</u> it's happening.

Who? What? Where? Nurse, the pills...

This is all fairly obvious really — the introduction gives a general idea of what's in the article, then you get the details. The next page shows you how these details are structured in the main text, before it's all nicely summed up in the conclusion. And they all lived happily ever after...

Structure

Let's face it, an article full of random info would be pretty hard to read. Which is why most articles link it all together into a neat little package.

The Body of the text is usually Structured in Paragraphs

Here's one common way of structuring an article:

1) The <u>main points</u> of a text are first given very briefly in the <u>introduction</u>.

2) Each <u>paragraph</u> of the <u>main body</u> of the text then <u>expands</u> on these ideas in turn.

Here's the main body of the whale article from the previous page:

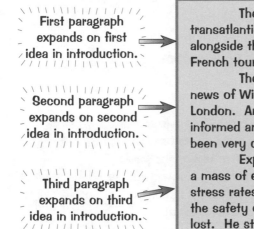

First paragraph expands on first idea in introduction.

Second paragraph expands on second idea in introduction.

Third paragraph expands on third idea in introduction.

> The whale, identified as a humpback that would normally be found in transatlantic waters, is bleeding from a wound to its side. It has been swimming alongside the Houses of Parliament all afternoon, having first been spotted by a French tourist who was walking the popular route.
>
> The number of onlookers has rapidly increased during the afternoon as news of Willy's sighting spread through the cafes, shops and offices of Central London. An unconfirmed source has reported that the Prime Minister has been informed and is being kept up to date with the unusual event. The crowd has also been very considerate of the whale's welfare by maintaining a quiet presence.
>
> Experts on marine biology arrived at the scene shortly after midday with a mass of equipment designed to measure and constantly record Willy's heart and stress rates. Dr John Tweed from University College commented on his fears for the safety of the whale because of his injuries and the amount of blood he has lost. He stated that his main priority was to return "Willy" to the open sea.

Conclusions summarise the Main Points

1) Conclusions give a <u>summary</u> of the <u>main points</u> of the article.

2) To be effective, they should leave the reader <u>thinking</u> about the <u>subject</u> of the article.

This summarises what was in the text.

This makes the reader think about their own attitudes.

> The questions that remain unanswered are how "Willy" came to be in the Thames and whether or not he will die, confirming the worst fears of most experts. However, the most intriguing question is why are we, as humans, so interested in his plight?

Write about conclusions Like This

Show that you understand that conclusions sum things up and remind the reader of the key points.

Show how the conclusion helps the reader to engage with the text.

> The conclusion sums up the main points of the article such as the views of the experts and their concerns that Willy will not survive. This ensures that the reader recalls the important details in the text.
>
> In addition, the last sentence, which asks the question as to why humans are so interested, encourages the reader to examine his or her own feelings on the subject.

And in conclusion, this is all dead easy...

So let me get this straight — the introduction's at the start and the conclusion's at the end, you say? You're absolutely sure about that then? Well, it's crazy, but it just might work...

P.E.E.D.

You can have loads of great ideas in your answers, but you won't get good marks unless you <u>explain</u> and <u>develop</u> them properly. That's where P.E.E.D. comes in — use it wisely my young apprentice...

P.E.E.D. stands for Point, Example, Explain, Develop

To write a good answer that gets you plenty of marks, you must do <u>four</u> things:

1)   Make a <u>point</u> to answer the question you've been given.

2)   Then give an <u>example</u> from the text (either a quote or a description).

3)   After that, <u>explain</u> how your example backs up your point.

4)   Finally, <u>develop</u> your point — this might involve saying what the <u>effect on the reader</u> is, saying what the <u>writer's intention</u> is, <u>linking</u> your point to another part of the text or giving your <u>own opinion</u>.

There are other versions of P.E.E.D. — P.E.E.R. (Point, Example, Explain, Relate), P.E.E.C.E. (Point, Example, Explain, Compare, Explore). The list goes on, but they all mean similar things.

There's more about how to do this on page 40.

Here's an example answer that includes those <u>four</u> things:

This is your <u>point</u>.

This bit is your <u>explanation</u>.

> The (writer feels quite angry about school dinners.) She says school food is ("pallid, tasteless pap".) The word "pap" has a disgusted sound to it. (It emphasises how appalled she is) at the low quality of the food. (I think the writer's intention is to show that) it isn't surprising that school dinners are unpopular. (She is implying that) schools should provide food that isn't disgusting if they want children to eat it.

This is your <u>example</u>.

This is where you <u>develop</u> your point further.

Explain what your example Shows about the Text

1)   Your example will usually be a <u>quote</u>, but it can also be a <u>reference</u>, e.g. a description of the pictures, font, layout or structure of the text. That's fine. It still counts as the example bit.

2)   The <u>explanation</u> and <u>development</u> parts are very important. They're your chance to show that you <u>really understand</u> and have <u>thought about</u> the text.

Here are some answers with different types of <u>examples</u>, clear <u>explanations</u> and <u>well-developed</u> points:

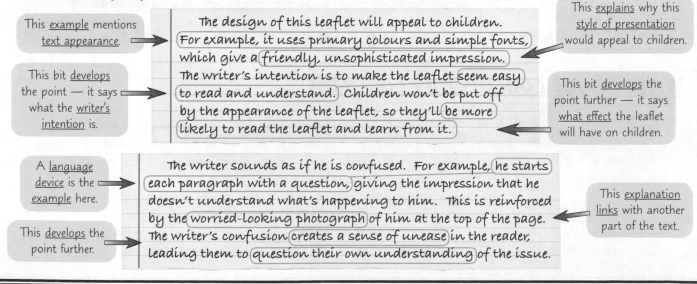

This <u>example</u> mentions <u>text appearance</u>.

This bit <u>develops</u> the point — it says what the <u>writer's intention</u> is.

> The design of this leaflet will appeal to children. (For example, it uses primary colours and simple fonts,) which give a (friendly, unsophisticated impression.) The writer's intention is to make the leaflet (seem easy) (to read and understand.) Children won't be put off by the appearance of the leaflet, so they'll (be more) (likely to read the leaflet and learn from it.)

This <u>explains</u> why this <u>style of presentation</u> would appeal to children.

This bit <u>develops</u> the point further — it says <u>what effect</u> the leaflet will have on children.

A <u>language device</u> is the <u>example</u> here.

This <u>develops</u> the point further.

> The writer sounds as if he is confused. For example, (he starts) (each paragraph with a question,) giving the impression that he doesn't understand what's happening to him. This is reinforced by the (worried-looking photograph) of him at the top of the page. The writer's confusion (creates a sense of unease) in the reader, leading them to (question their own understanding) of the issue.

This <u>explanation</u> <u>links</u> with another part of the text.

Would you like to share the joke with the rest of the class?

Getting P.E.E.D. into your head is pretty important — it'll help you to remember how to get those top marks. So, always remember to check you've P.E.E.D. on your work (sorry, couldn't resist).

Writing in Paragraphs

I'm sure you know about paragraphs already so I'm not going to go on about how to write in paragraphs. But you do need to know why it's so important.

Paragraphs are a good way to Structure Your Answer

1) Here's some fun examiner jargon — you've got to "develop and sustain" your theories about texts. This means that you've got to make several detailed points in your answers.

2) You need to organise your points clearly and link them together — and the best way to do that is to write in paragraphs.

3) You can use different paragraph structures to organise your points in different ways. For example:

  • You could write a paragraph for every point you want to make, and each paragraph could have a P.E.E.D. structure (see previous page).

  • You could make two points that contrast or agree with each other within a paragraph — this can be useful when writing about arguments (see pages 12 and 13).

  • You could make one point and link together lots of examples with different explanations within a paragraph.

However you structure your paragraphs, make sure you include all the parts of P.E.E.D. somewhere in your answer.

How you Link Your Paragraphs is important

Linking your paragraphs together smoothly is an important skill — it makes your writing look more confident and better thought out.

1) The beginning of a paragraph needs to show what the paragraph is about. Link it to key words in the question.

The writer creates an immediate sense of anger through the headlines she chooses.

This makes it clear you're answering a question about how the writer shows anger.

2) You might want to link a new paragraph with a previous paragraph.

This is not the only way in which the writer shows bias.

This refers back to the paragraph you've just finished.

3) You could show you're moving on to another topic.

The writer's choice of fonts is also important.

This introduces your new topic.

4) You might be introducing a comparison or contrast with a previous paragraph.

Although the first paragraph uses lots of questions, the rest of the article sounds much more definite.

This word helps you start writing about a difference.

See page 12 for some more examples of linking words and phrases.

Make a chart of tropical birds — draw a parrotgraph...

This stuff kind of comes naturally when you've had enough practice. So keep doing practice exams and answering practice questions — pretty soon you'll be producing beautiful answers.

Reading with Insight

Reading with insight is what the examiners call a 'higher order' reading skill. That means you have to show you can do it to get the higher grades — especially when you're asked to discuss or comment.

You need to look Beyond what's Obvious

Reading with insight helps you to <u>develop</u> your points — that's the 'D' in P.E.E.D. (see p.38).

You may understand the facts a writer gives you, but you'll need to write about <u>more</u> than just those facts in your answers.

1) You can show <u>insight</u> if you work out what a writer's <u>attitude</u> is. For example:

> There is a strong sense that the writer feels angry about the changes.

2) You could show you understand <u>what</u> the writer wants readers to <u>think about</u>. For example:

> The article makes the reader question whether schools are a good thing.

3) You could comment on how the writer tries to make readers <u>feel</u>. For example:

> The writer seems to want to make readers feel guilty.

4) You might write about <u>why</u> you think a piece was written. For example:

> Perhaps the writer felt he needed to make sure the memory of his friend was kept alive.

5) You could comment on any <u>changes</u> to the writer's <u>argument</u> or <u>language</u> <u>style</u> within the text. For example:

> The writer uses a serious, formal tone to describe the new exam rules, but then changes to a more informal, light-hearted style to wish students good luck in their exams.

The Examiner wants to hear Your Opinion

You can get marks for giving thoughtful <u>personal opinions</u>. Make sure you focus on the <u>text</u> though — examiners don't want to know your general opinions on various unrelated issues.

THIS WOULD BE GOOD:

> I think the article would remind older people of happier times because it includes so many descriptive details.

THIS WOULD BE BAD:

> I think old people are quite boring.

Examiners love Alternative Interpretations

If you give <u>more than one</u> possible way of <u>looking</u> at a text, the examiner will be extremely impressed. For example:

> The short sentences could give an impression of anxiety and tension, or they could suggest to some readers that the writer has an arrogant attitude.

This shows that you've got plenty of ideas.

Make sure you're reading with insight of a cup of tea...

There's lots of really good advice on this page. I'd read it over one more time if I were you. You've got to show some insight, give your opinion, and give different interpretations, if you can.

Reading with Insight

If you're after those high grades, you've got to go a bit further than finding facts. You'll need to work out what writers are <u>implying</u> too. This is where <u>inference</u> and <u>empathy</u> come in.

Inference means working things out from Clues

Writers don't always make things obvious. You can use <u>evidence</u> in the text to work out what the writer <u>really</u> wants us to think. Make sure you use <u>details</u> from the text though. Don't just guess.

1) <u>Language</u> gives you clues.

> The writer uses words like "endless" and "unoriginal", which imply that he did not enjoy the film.

This shows you have made an inference.

2) You can draw inferences from <u>pictures</u>.

> The article appears to be critical of the circus because it includes pictures of cramped animal cages and fields full of litter.

You can use this phrase to infer too.

3) Text <u>details</u> give you hints.

> The writer gives a sense of being biased in favour of the exam system because she only uses examples of successful candidates.

This phrase shows there's another deduction coming up.

It's useful to work out the Writer's Tone

Obviously, you can't actually hear the writer's tone of voice. But the <u>language</u> in the text can give away the writer's <u>emotions</u> and <u>attitudes</u> — and that's called <u>tone</u> too.

Here's an answer that mentions the writer's <u>tone</u>:

> The writer sounds sarcastic when she calls the contestants "the finest brains the country could scrape together."

This bit comments on tone.

See p. 10-11 for more on tone.

You can Show Empathy with the writer

1) Empathy means showing you <u>understand</u> how the writer <u>feels</u>.
2) You could make a <u>link</u> between the <u>writer's experiences</u> and <u>your own</u>.
3) <u>Don't</u> give too much <u>detail</u> about yourself though. The examiner's only interested in your understanding of the <u>text</u> — not your life story.

   Here's a good example:

Sandra preferred to show empathy with dolphins.

Use phrases like this to show empathy.

> The writer seems to be anxious and restless, just like I would feel before an exam.
> It must have been uncomfortable for him.

He snored loudly, giving the sense that he was bored...

Don't worry if some of these techniques sound a bit tricky. There are lots of different ways to show insight. Most questions have more than one right answer — that's what makes English such fun...

Search and Find Questions

The simplest type of exam question asks you to pick out particular information from a text. Here are some tips on how to answer them well...

Some questions ask you to Pick Out Information

1) These questions test your ability to <u>understand</u> the text, <u>select</u> relevant <u>information</u> and <u>order</u> it into a <u>coherent</u> answer.

2) Here's an example:

> Read **Item 1**, the article called *Homecoming* by Betty Munro.
> **1** What do you learn from the article about why Melrose is a wonderful place to live?
>
> *(8 marks)*

3) This type of question is fairly straightforward — but you need to make sure you find <u>all</u> the <u>relevant details</u> and write about them <u>clearly</u> to get <u>top marks</u>.

Read the text Carefully

1) After you've read the exam question, <u>look back through</u> the <u>text</u>.

2) As you read, <u>underline</u> information that <u>answers the question</u>.
   E.g. here's part of the text that goes with the exam question above:

> At the age of 46, I was fed up of London. I sold my house and rented a cottage in the <u>idyllic</u> Scottish town where I grew up. After just a few weeks, I knew I'd made the right decision: Melrose, with its <u>friendly people</u> and <u>stunning scenery</u>, is where my heart is and it's a wonderful place to live.
> It is <u>terribly pretty</u>, with the kind of <u>charming</u>, local shops that are rapidly being replaced by supermarket giants elsewhere. For such a tiny place, it is <u>buzzing with life</u>. There's a <u>theatre</u>, <u>museum</u> and literary society. The <u>sporting facilities</u> are fantastic, with an excellent rugby pitch.

It's important to Keep your answer Focused

1) Select the parts of the text that <u>answer the question best</u> — don't include any extra waffle.

2) You can use <u>short quotes</u>, or explain what the writer says <u>in your own words</u>. If you use quotes, remember to use <u>quotation marks</u>.

3) Avoid quoting <u>long chunks</u> — it gives the examiner the impression that you <u>don't understand</u> the text and can't tell which bits are most important.

4) All the points you make should be <u>based on the text</u> and <u>help to answer the question</u>.

THIS WOULD BE GOOD:

The writer says Melrose is "terribly pretty" and has "charming" shops. She is also enthusiastic about the sporting facilities, for example the "excellent" rugby field.

THIS WOULD BE BAD:

The writer says that at the age of 46, she was fed up of London. She must have been bored of cities. She seems to think Melrose is much better than London, probably because it's rural.

Where could you find a question? — Search me....

With 'search and find' questions it's important to follow the text closely, and pick out all the relevant points. Don't get sidetracked. Save your skills of insight and evaluation for the trickier questions...

Comparing Texts

In the exam, there will be a question that asks you to <u>compare two texts</u>. For example, you might have to compare the way they are written or how they are presented. These questions can be tricky — so here's a page of hints about how to tackle them...

Plan your answer Before you start Writing

Here's a <u>question</u> that asks you to compare two texts:

Now you need to refer to **Item 1**, the magazine article called *Teen Times* and **Item 2**, the newspaper article *Youth Out of Control*.

1   Compare the two articles. In your answer you should mention:

- the writers' intended audiences
- what the writers say about young people
- the ways in which the writers use language.

And here's how you could <u>plan</u> an answer to that question:

Set your notes out in lists, side by side, to help you compare.

Each line of notes matches a bullet point or key word in the question.

Item 1
Audience — teenagers
Examples of achievements
Uses slang, enthusiastic tone

Item 2
Audience — adult readers
Examples of bad behaviour
Formal, critical, emotive language

Try to Compare the texts as you Go Along

Here's part of a <u>possible answer</u> to the question above:

Write about both texts in the same paragraph.

This introduces a difference.

This introduces your example.

The author of Item 1 is writing for a teenage audience, whereas Item 2 is for a general adult readership. This is partly suggested by the appearance of each text. Item 1 uses an informal looking font and illustrates the piece with cartoons, creating a sense of youth and energy. Item 2, on the other hand, is set out in traditional newspaper columns with a small font size, which suggests that it is aimed at adults.

Although both pieces are about teenagers, the texts differ in the way they refer to young people; the headline in Item 1 uses the word "we", while Item 2 refers to teenagers as "they". This shows that Item 1 tries to identify with youngsters, while Item 2 does not.

This is the explanation bit.

This points out a similarity.

Here's another difference.

Next up, all the way from Bolton — oh you said "compare"

Make sure you include loads of cross-references — go back and forth between texts so that you're always comparing. Here are some words that'll help: "similarly", "despite", "in contrast to", "just as", "equally", "alternatively", "in the same way" and "likewise". Try to memorise a few of these.

Summary of the Exam

I bet you're just aching to know all about your exam. Well, the next two pages tell you what the exam's going to be like and how long you should spend on the different bits. Fun fun fun.

The Exam's in Two Sections

1) Whether you're doing <u>GCSE English Language</u> or <u>GCSE English</u>, you only have to do <u>one exam</u>.

2) It's the <u>same</u> exam for both courses, and it's for <u>Unit 1: Understanding and producing non-fiction texts</u>.

3) You get <u>2 hours 15 minutes</u> for the exam. Here's how it's <u>structured</u>:

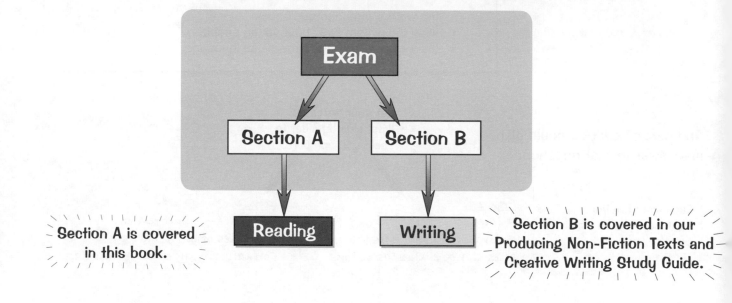

Section A is covered in this book.

Section B is covered in our Producing Non-Fiction Texts and Creative Writing Study Guide.

The Front Page tells you What To Do

First up — <u>what to do</u> when you plonk yourself down in that nice, comfy exam chair (there's more on the <u>structure</u> of the exam on the next page):

1) The <u>front page</u> of the exam paper tells you what you should have in front of you. Read it through and make sure you've <u>got everything</u>.
   - There will be a <u>main exam paper</u> which will have all the <u>questions</u> and <u>space</u> to write your <u>answers</u>.
   - You'll also have a <u>separate insert</u> containing <u>three non-fiction texts</u>.

2) Make sure you fill in all the <u>details</u> you're asked for on the <u>front</u> of the exam paper, or you won't get any marks at all — not ideal.

3) Make sure you've got the <u>higher tier</u> paper, not the foundation one.

4) Read all the <u>instructions and tips</u> on the front page, to remind you what to do.

My mum tells me what to do...

So there you are, one lovely exam on non-fiction texts and that's Unit 1 sorted. All we're looking at in this book is the first part of the exam (understanding non-fiction texts, also known as reading), but it's good to know where it fits in with the other part (producing non-fiction texts, or writing).

Summary of the Exam

This page is about the different <u>questions</u>, and how many <u>marks</u> each one's worth. Crikey, with all this info to take in about the exam, they'll be giving you an exam on the exam next...

Section A and Section B are Both Worth 40 Marks

1) The whole exam is worth <u>80 marks</u>, and counts for <u>40%</u> of your total GCSE mark (for both GCSE English Language and GCSE English).

2) You can get up to <u>40 marks</u> for <u>Section A</u> and <u>40 marks</u> for <u>Section B</u>.

3) Section A will have <u>four</u> questions — <u>three</u> worth <u>8 marks</u> and <u>one</u> worth <u>16 marks</u>.

4) Section B will have <u>two</u> questions — <u>one</u> worth <u>16 marks</u> and the other worth <u>24 marks</u>.

Section A is based on *Three Pieces* of Non-Fiction Text

1) The <u>four</u> questions in Section A will be based on <u>3 pieces of non-fiction text</u> that you haven't seen before — they'll be in the <u>insert</u> you're given in the exam.

2) You'll need to use <u>one</u> of the texts for <u>each</u> of the first <u>three questions</u>. So question one will be on <u>item one</u>, question two will be on <u>item two</u> and question three will be on <u>item three</u>.

In his exam, James was faced with a type of text he had never seen before.

3) Question four will be a <u>comparison</u> question — you'll have to compare two of the three texts. You'll be <u>told</u> one of the texts you have to write about, but you can <u>choose</u> the other for yourself.

4) Make sure you read the questions properly so that your answer is about the <u>right text or texts</u>.

Answer All the Questions

1) You have to answer <u>every question</u> in this exam.

2) You should spend about <u>1 hour 15 minutes</u> on Section A and <u>1 hour</u> on Section B. The time you spend on Section A needs to include time to <u>read the texts</u> you've been given.

> It's best to spend about <u>5 minutes reading each text</u> (15 minutes in total), and <u>1 hour writing your answers</u> to Section A — this leaves you with about an hour for Section B.

3) The amount of <u>marks</u> each question is worth affects how much <u>time</u> you should spend on each question — the <u>more marks</u> a question is worth, the <u>more time</u> you should spend on it.

4) In Section A, the first <u>three</u> questions are worth <u>8 marks</u> each — aim to spend about <u>12 minutes</u> on each one. The <u>fourth</u> question is worth <u>16 marks</u>, so try and spend about <u>24 minutes</u> on it.

That's the theory sorted — turn over to see an exam...

Now you know how the exam is structured, I bet you're dying to have a look at an actual paper. Well, I was feeling nice today so I made one just for you — take a look at the next few pages.

Exam Paper — Questions

Here are some lovely <u>example questions</u> — similar to the ones you'll get in Section A of your Unit 1 exam. The texts are printed on the next three pages (in the exam they'll be in a separate insert).

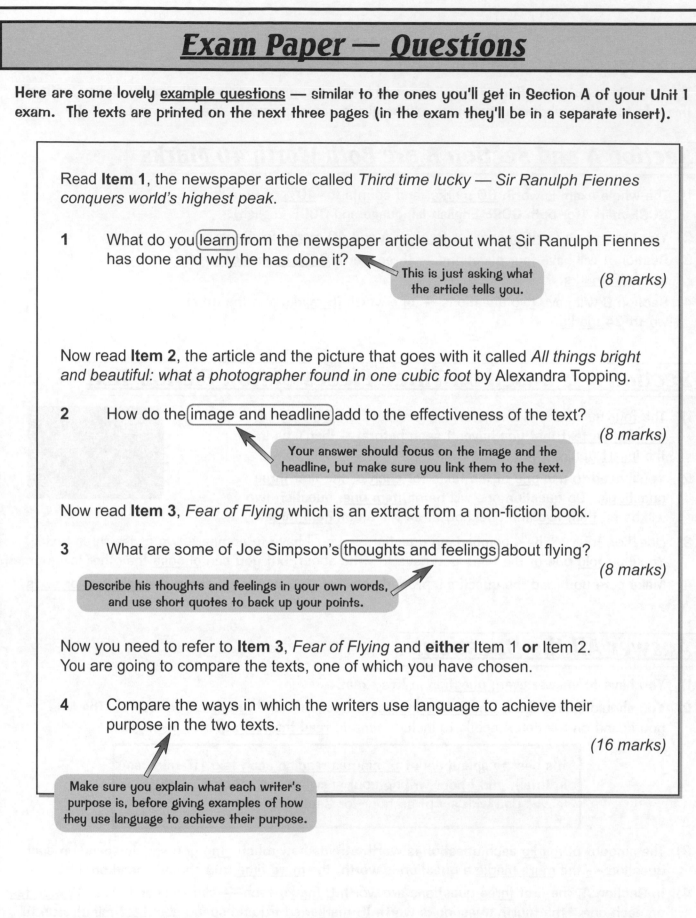

Read **Item 1**, the newspaper article called *Third time lucky — Sir Ranulph Fiennes conquers world's highest peak*.

1   What do you learn from the newspaper article about what Sir Ranulph Fiennes has done and why he has done it?

This is just asking what the article tells you.

(8 marks)

Now read **Item 2**, the article and the picture that goes with it called *All things bright and beautiful: what a photographer found in one cubic foot* by Alexandra Topping.

2   How do the image and headline add to the effectiveness of the text?

(8 marks)

Your answer should focus on the image and the headline, but make sure you link them to the text.

Now read **Item 3**, *Fear of Flying* which is an extract from a non-fiction book.

3   What are some of Joe Simpson's thoughts and feelings about flying?

(8 marks)

Describe his thoughts and feelings in your own words, and use short quotes to back up your points.

Now you need to refer to **Item 3**, *Fear of Flying* and **either** Item 1 **or** Item 2. You are going to compare the texts, one of which you have chosen.

4   Compare the ways in which the writers use language to achieve their purpose in the two texts.

(16 marks)

Make sure you explain what each writer's purpose is, before giving examples of how they use language to achieve their purpose.

"How did you find the exam?" "It was just on the table..."

It's important to look at sample exam questions like this to get an idea of what the real exam is like. One thing you'll notice — certain types of question come up again and again: compare this, what do you learn from that, what are some of this person's thoughts and feelings...

Exam Source — Item 1

Here's Item 1 — one of your texts for the exam questions on page 46.

Third time lucky — Sir Ranulph Fiennes conquers world's highest peak

21st May 2009

After two unsuccessful attempts, Sir Ranulph Fiennes has finally made it to the summit of Everest — the world's highest mountain.

The 65-year old reached the summit just before 1am (British time) on Thursday 21st May 2009, and became the oldest British man to make it to the top of the Himalayan mountain (and the first British pensioner).

This latest success means that Sir Ranulph is the first man to cross both the north and south poles and conquer Mount Everest.

The life-long adventurer climbed Everest to raise money for the cancer charity Marie Curie, for which he has already raised millions of pounds.

Sir Ranulph said: "I have summited Everest for Marie Curie Cancer Care which has long been a personal goal.

"I urge everyone who followed my attempt last year to give generously to Marie Curie so that we can at last achieve our £3 million target to support its pioneering work in end-of-life care."

He started this expedition to Everest three weeks ago, but wanted to keep the trip quiet, having failed to reach the summit during his previous two attempts (in 2005 and 2008).

Sir Ranulph had already had a triple heart bypass for a heart attack he suffered in 2003. He then suffered another heart attack during his 2005 attempt to conquer Everest (at 8,500 metres). He recovered and decided to try again in 2008 but had to turn back at 8,400 metres, suffering from exhaustion.

After his 2008 attempt he said: "I won't be returning to Everest. It's a seven week trip — last time I had a heart attack, this time bad timing and weather scuppered my chances. I think any third attempt would be bad luck."

However, it proved to be third time lucky — he changed his mind and went on to conquer the 8,850 metre peak.

This new success adds to the long list of Sir Ranulph's achievements. He was the first man to reach the north and south poles by land unaided. In 2003, he completed seven marathons on seven continents in seven days and in 2007 he climbed the notoriously dangerous north face of the Eiger.

The recent BBC2 series 'Top Dogs' brought Sir Ranulph Fiennes, solo yachtsman Sir Robin Knox-Johnston and BBC world affairs editor John Simpson together as they sailed around Cape Horn, trekked across the Arctic and filed war reports from Afghanistan.

Marie Curie is a charity that is particularly close to Sir Ranulph's heart, as his first wife, sister and mother all died of cancer within 18 months of each other.

Thomas Hughes-Hallett, the chief executive of Marie Curie said: "Everyone at Marie Curie is delighted that Sir Ranulph has conquered Everest. We know it meant so much to him — we are so grateful to Ran for all his support for the charity and for his determination to personally take the Marie Curie flag to the summit."

Exam Source — Item 2

Here's Item 2 — another text for those fun-looking exam questions on page 46.

All things bright and beautiful: what a photographer found in one cubic foot

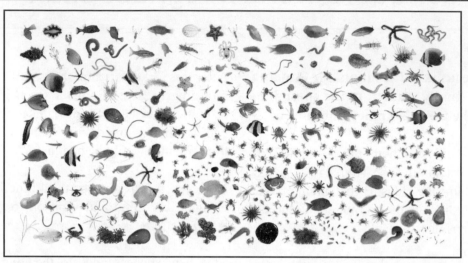

'It was like finding little gems' — just some of the creatures photographed by David Liittschwager for National Geographic. Photograph: David Liittschwager/National Geographic Stock

Alexandra Topping
Sunday 24th January 2010
guardian.co.uk

Just how much life can you find in an ecosystem of one cubic foot? That is the question photographer David Liittschwager set out to answer when he took a 12-inch metal frame to a range of different environments on land and in water, in tropical climes and temperate regions and began to chart the living organisms.

The answer? An astonishing amount. In each place he visited, the photographer, best known for his large images of rare animals and plants, was amazed at the diversity and abundance of life that passed through such a small area.

In five distinct and contrasting environments, from a tropical forest to a city-centre park, Liittschwager set down his green-edged metal cube, and started watching. Each creature that passed through the cube was counted and charted with the help of his assistant and a team of biologists. Over a three-week period the team photographed each inhabitant that passed through the cube, down to creatures measuring a mere millimetre.

In total, more than a thousand individual organisms were photographed, and the diversity of each environment can be seen on nationalgeographic.com. "It was like finding little gems," Liittschwager said.

The team started out at Central Park in New York – or more specifically, in the Hallet nature sanctuary, a 3.5-acre deciduous woodland area, populated with trees or shrubs that lose their leaves seasonally. There they found the tufted titmouse and eastern grey squirrel, creatures as big as a raccoon and as small as a leopard slug.

In Moorea, in French Polynesia, they discovered a vast array of species (pictured) thought to only be a very small selection of the reef's full diversity. Among their findings were the inch-long file clam, the whitespotted boxfish, sacoglossan sea slug and the frankly terrifying post-larval octopus.

While in the tropical cloud forest of Monteverde, in Costa Rica, most of the animals in the treetop ecosystem were as small as a fingertip; there were hawk moths, sharpshooter leafhoppers and burio tree seeds.

The fine-leaved vegetation of the fynbos of Table Mountain in South Africa, thought to hold one of the richest concentrations of plant diversity in the world, revealed the purple flower of the alice sundew, and no shortage of cape zebra cockroaches. Finally, in the fresh water of Duck River in Tennessee, one of the most biodiverse waterways in the US, swam golden darters and longlear sunfish as well as the bigeyed chub.

Exam Source — Item 3

This is Item 3 — the third piece of text you need to answer the exam questions.

Fear of Flying

In this extract, Joe Simpson, a famous mountaineer and writer, is remembering how he developed a fear of flying.

To put it mildly, I dislike flying. Since I spend a lot of time travelling around the world, this is rather inconvenient. Once, when flying from Islamabad to London, I was so overcome with anxiety that shortly after take-off I found myself locked in the lavatory, braced across the seat with my legs jammed against the sink unit, in a state close to hysteria. I believe this irrational fear stemmed from a terrifying landing in Germany on a rainswept windy night in 1974. I was fourteen, and sitting by the window with my eldest brother, David, beside me as we approached the runway. I watched the wing dipping and yawing alarmingly as we flew through gusts of crosswind. David seemed quite unperturbed by the conditions and calmly read his book. Up to then I had happily accepted that flying was the safest way to travel and that the probability of ever knowing someone who had been involved in an air crash, let alone experiencing it myself, was so small as to be not worth worrying about.

I watched the runway lights appear out of the gloomy darkness. They were fixed to box-shaped metal poles at intervals along the edge of the tarmac. As the ground rushed up towards us I sat back and waited for the smooth rumble as the undercarriage met the concrete. Suddenly we dropped with a stomach emptying swoop and hit the runway with shocking force. I felt the impact of it thudding up through my seat. There was a loud bang and the aircraft bounced back into the air before lurching drunkenly down again on to the tarmac. After we struck the second time we seemed to be tearing along on two wheels, canted steeply over on my side. The overhead lockers flew open, the lights went out, and many of the passengers started screaming and shouting. Flight bags, coats and bottles of duty free gin and whiskey cascaded down from the lockers.

I remember staring fixedly out of the window, watching the wing tip dipping towards the runway lights that were flashing past with frightening speed. I was convinced they were going to hit the wing, and I knew enough about wings full of fuel and high velocity impacts to guess what would happen if they did.

I didn't scream, and nor did David, but in the brief moment of darkness I clearly heard adult males yelling in panic. Frightened as I was, I remember thinking that men were not supposed to scream; at least, they never did so in films. It was unnerving to hear. Suddenly the plane righted itself, the reverse thrust of the engines began to brake our hurtling charge, and the lights came back on. Within seconds we were taxiing down the runway at walking speed.

Mark Scheme

Ever thought, "If only I could get inside that examiner's head"? Not literally of course, that would be hideous. But these pages will show you just how they'd mark the exam questions on page 46 — so that you know exactly what to do to please them. Ooh, isn't it subversive...

Question 1

> Read **Item 1**, the newspaper article called *Third time lucky — Sir Ranulph Fiennes conquers world's highest peak*.
>
> 1   What do you learn from the newspaper article about what Sir Ranulph Fiennes has done and why he has done it?
>
> (8 marks)

The table below shows how the quality of your answer is related to the number of marks you get. Obviously, all answers are different and it's unlikely that any one answer will fit exactly into all three columns for a particular mark band — it's a question of finding the 'best fit'.

Number of marks	What you've written	How you've written	How your answer's put together
Band 1 1-2 marks	Limited description of what you've read with a couple of basic points, not really answering the question.	Confusingly written showing limited understanding of the text. Sections of the text may be copied.	No clear structure — points are in a random order.
Band 2 3-4 marks	Some points made that attempt to answer the question, but not balanced between what Fiennes did and why he did it. Offers some relevant quotations.	More clearly written showing some understanding of the text and mostly in own words.	An attempt at a loose structure (e.g. first writing about what he's done, then why) but not always kept to.
Band 3 5-6 marks	Several clear points made about both parts of the question, with relevant use of quotations.	Clearly written showing a good understanding of the text. Own words used throughout answer.	Clear structure (e.g. first writing about what he's done, then why). Some points may be linked together making it easy to follow.
Band 4 7-8 marks	Detailed points made linking together what Fiennes did and why he did it. Thoughtful use of relevant quotations.	Clear, confident, detailed summary showing a full understanding of the text.	Well structured, with points connecting together so that the answer is fluent and easy to follow.

Mark Scheme

In my day of course they just rolled some dice or prayed to the Greek gods to decide what grade we got. It's a bit more sophisticated now though. Here's how they'd mark question 2.

Question 2

> Now read **Item 2**, the article and the picture that goes with it called *All things bright and beautiful: what a photographer found in one cubic foot* by Alexandra Topping.
>
> 2   How do the image and headline add to the effectiveness of the text?
>
> *(8 marks)*

Number of marks	What you've written	How you've written	How your answer's put together
Band 1 1-2 marks	Limited explanation of the meaning of the headline and what the image shows. No link made between the image and headline and the text.	Confusingly written, may copy large sections of the text out.	No clear structure — points are in a random order and aren't linked together.
Band 2 3-4 marks	Some points made showing that you've understood the purpose of the headline and the image. Some attempt made to link the image and headline to the text.	More clearly written, mostly in own words.	An attempt at a loose structure (e.g. first talking about the image, then talking about the headline) but not always kept to.
Band 3 5-6 marks	Clear explanation of the purpose of the headline and the image, showing how they add to the effectiveness of the text.	Clearly written, with own words used throughout.	Clear structure (e.g. first explaining the image and headline, then commenting on how they add to the effectiveness of the text), through most of answer.
Band 4 7-8 marks	Detailed and thoughtful interpretation of the headline and the image, showing clearly why they are appropriate and how they add to the effectiveness of the text.	Clear and detailed summary with confident use of technical terms (e.g. metaphor, simile etc.).	Well structured with points about the headline, image and text linked together to make a fluent description of how they work together.

Mark Scheme

And you thought marking exams was just like choosing lottery numbers. Nope, it requires quite a lot more thought and effort. Here's the mark scheme for question 3.

Question 3

Now read **Item 3**, *Fear of Flying* which is an extract from a non-fiction book.

3   What are some of Joe Simpson's thoughts and feelings about flying?

(8 marks)

Number of marks	What you've written	How you've written	How your answer's put together
Band 1 1-2 marks	Limited description of the text with little reference to the thoughts and feelings about flying.	Confusingly written, possibly with whole sections of the text copied out.	No clear structure — points are in a random order.
Band 2 3-4 marks	Some points made showing you've understood some of the author's thoughts and feelings about flying. Some quotes used to support points.	More clearly written, mostly in own words showing some understanding of the text.	Some points are linked together to give the answer a loose structure.
Band 3 5-6 marks	Clear explanation of the thoughts and feelings that the writer states and shows through his writing. Relevant quotes used to back up clear points.	Clearly written showing a good understanding of the text and using own words throughout answer.	Clear structure with most points linked together so it's easy to follow.
Band 4 7-8 marks	Detailed and thoughtful interpretation of the thoughts and feelings stated and implied by the writer. Relevant quotes used to back up detailed points.	Detailed summary showing a full understanding of the text with confident use of technical terms.	Well-structured, with thoughts and feelings discussed in a fluent way.

Mark Scheme

Question 4

> Now you need to refer to **Item 3**, *Fear of Flying* and **either** Item 1 **or** Item 2.
> You are going to compare the texts, one of which you have chosen.
>
> 4   Compare the ways in which the writers use language to achieve their purpose in the two texts.
>
> *(16 marks)*

Number of marks	What you've written	How you've written	How your answer's put together
Band 1 1-4 marks	One or two brief points about language with no real comparison and very few examples.	Confusingly written, showing limited understanding of purpose or use of language.	No clear structure. Points are not linked together or cross-referenced.
Band 2 5-8 marks	A few points about the effect of language, backed up with examples. Some attempt to compare the items.	More clearly written showing some understanding of purpose and use of language.	Loose structure (e.g. first talking about one text then comparing it to the other) but not always kept to.
Band 3 9-12 marks	Several clear points discussing purpose and use of language, backed up with relevant examples. Clear comparisons made between the texts.	Clearly written showing a good understanding of purpose and use of language. Own words used throughout answer.	Clear structure (e.g. first talking about one text then comparing it to the other) throughout most of the answer, with points linked together.
Band 4 13-16 marks	Thoughtful, detailed points, backed up by relevant quotes, about how the writers have used language differently to achieve their purpose.	Clear, confident and detailed comparison, showing a full understanding of purpose and use of language.	Clear and consistent structure with points cross-referenced to make accurate comparisons.

How they work out your Grade

Add up the marks from the four questions and use the table below to get your mock exam grade. (The grade boundaries vary slightly from year to year, but this is a good general guide.)

Marks	20-23	24-27	28-31	32-35	36-40
Grade	D	C	B	A	A*

Of course, your final GCSE grade is an average of this and the rest of your Unit 1 Exam, Unit 2 and Unit 3. But the grade you get from this section shows the grade you're on course for.

Grade C & B Answers to Question 1

These two pages show you different grade answers to question 1 — starting with a C grade answer and working up to an A*. Look back at pages 46-49 for the exam questions and texts.

Think about what the article is Really Telling Us

1) Read the question through a couple of times so you're really sure of what to do.

2) You're looking for information about what Sir Ranulph has done and why he has done it — so make sure you cover both parts of the question.

Here's a "C" grade answer to the question.

> Sir Ranulph Fiennes has recently climbed Everest, making him the first man to cross both the north and south poles and conquer Mount Everest. Sir Ranulph Fiennes had tried to climb Everest before, two times, but had failed, then he succeeded in getting to the top on his third attempt. He kept trying to climb Everest because he wanted to raise money for his favourite charity. He said "I have summited Everest for Marie Curie Cancer Care".

This is an accurate point but use your own words.

This needs more detail about when he attempted to climb Everest before, and why he failed.

Quote is used to support the point, but it should be explained in more detail, i.e. why he chose to support Marie Curie.

This answer is a start — the information in it is accurate, but it needs to include more detail about what Sir Ranulph Fiennes did and why he did it.

Use lots of Evidence to back up your points

1) Try to use your own words instead of just copying bits of the text — this shows that you've thought about what you're writing.

2) Back up your points with lots of short, snappy quotes.

Here's a "B" grade answer to the question.

Beatrice was really good at snappy quotes.

> At the age of 65, Sir Ranulph Fiennes reached the world's "highest peak" as he conquered Everest. This makes him the "oldest British man" and "first British pensioner" to climb Everest. Sir Ranulph had made two previous unsuccessful attempts to conquer the mountain, the first was unsuccessful as he had a heart attack and he failed the second time because he became exhausted. This recent success is the latest in a long line of achievements: he has also reached both "the north and south poles by land unaided" and climbed "the notoriously dangerous north face of the Eiger".
> He climbed Everest because he wanted to raise money for Marie Curie Cancer Care. The article tells us Sir Ranulph Fiennes lost three members of his family to cancer.

Good use of short quotes within the sentences.

Good detail about his previous attempts but the sentence could be less rambling.

This tells us why he did it, but it's a bit brief.

This answer covers the first part of the question in a lot of detail, but only touches on the second. You should cover what he did and why he did it equally to get higher marks.

Grade A & A* Answers to Question 1

You need to show a Very Good Understanding of the article

1) You should show you've understood <u>all</u> the <u>key points</u> in the article.

2) Your quotations and evidence should really <u>add</u> to what you're saying, not just prove it.

3) Plan your answer to make it <u>well-structured</u> and <u>relevant</u> to the question.

Here's an "<u>A</u>" <u>grade</u> answer to question 1.

> The main point that the reader learns from the article is that Sir Ranulph Fiennes has "finally made it" to the top of Mount Everest on his third attempt. The first time Fiennes attempted to climb Everest was in 2005 but he "suffered another heart attack" at 8,500m. He tried again in 2008, but had to "turn back at 8,400m" because he had become exhausted. After his second attempt he said "I won't be returning to Everest". But he did try again, and was successful. Because the article tells us about all three attempts, we learn that Fiennes was very determined to summit Everest.
> We also learn about why Sir Fiennes was so determined to do what he did. He did it to raise "£3 million" for Marie Curie Cancer Care, but he also had personal reasons for supporting that particular charity. The article tells us that "his first wife, sister and mother all died of cancer". This shows why his determination to reach the summit of Everest was so great.

Gets straight to the point of the article.

Clear structure — one paragraph for what Fiennes has done, and one for why.

This is a bit vague.

Links nicely to the previous paragraph.

Link your points together Fluently

1) Your answer should <u>clearly</u> and <u>concisely</u> describe what you <u>learn</u> from the article.

2) You need to cover <u>both</u> parts of the question <u>thoroughly</u>.

Here's an "<u>A*</u>" <u>grade</u> answer to question 1.

> From this article, we learn about Sir Ranulph Fiennes' successful conquest of Everest, from which he hopes to raise "£3 million" for charity. The article tells us that he has twice attempted to climb Everest before; his 2005 attempt had to be abandoned after he "suffered another heart attack" (following an earlier heart attack and heart surgery), and in 2008 he had to turn back "suffering from exhaustion". This shows his determination and drive: he didn't let a number of potentially dangerous setbacks prevent him from reaching his goal. His physical and mental strength is further highlighted by the other achievements that are mentioned in the article, for example, he has also "completed seven marathons on seven continents in seven days", as well as being the first man to "reach the north and south poles by land unaided".
> We also learn what Sir Ranulph's motivation was: he wanted to support the cancer charity Marie Curie in its "pioneering work in end-of-life care". The charity is "close to Sir Ranulph's heart"; we learn that "his first wife, sister and mother all died of cancer", which makes us sympathise with and admire him. It also gives us a better understanding of why Fiennes was so determined to climb Everest: he wanted to "personally take the Marie Curie flag to the summit", perhaps in memory of his family, but also to help others who are suffering from cancer.

Opening sentence sums up entire article.

Develops the point well.

More points about what he did are nicely linked together.

Makes inferences about the author's motivation.

This is a <u>clear answer</u> with plenty of <u>detail</u> and good use of <u>P.E.E.D.</u> (see p.38).

Grade C & B Answers to Question 2

Well, that's question 1 done, now for <u>question 2</u>. Remember, the exam's on pages 46-49.

Focus on the Image and the Headline

1) As usual, <u>read through</u> the question a couple of times so you're sure what to do.

2) You need to focus on the <u>image</u> and the <u>headline</u>.

3) It's not enough to just show that you understand the image and headline — you have to say how they <u>connect</u> with the text.

Here's a <u>"C" grade</u> answer to question 2.

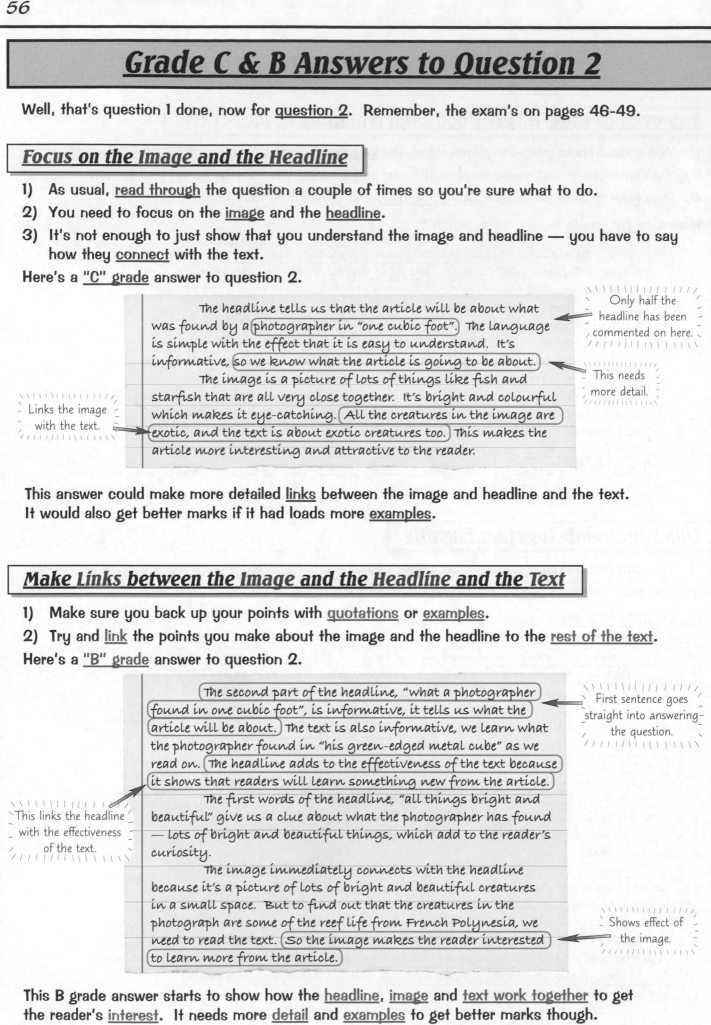

The headline tells us that the article will be about what was found by a photographer in "one cubic foot". The language is simple with the effect that it is easy to understand. It's informative, so we know what the article is going to be about.

The image is a picture of lots of things like fish and starfish that are all very close together. It's bright and colourful which makes it eye-catching. All the creatures in the image are exotic, and the text is about exotic creatures too. This makes the article more interesting and attractive to the reader.

Only half the headline has been commented on here.

This needs more detail.

Links the image with the text.

This answer could make more detailed <u>links</u> between the image and headline and the text. It would also get better marks if it had loads more <u>examples</u>.

Make Links between the Image and the Headline and the Text

1) Make sure you back up your points with <u>quotations</u> or <u>examples</u>.

2) Try and <u>link</u> the points you make about the image and the headline to the <u>rest of the text</u>.

Here's a <u>"B" grade</u> answer to question 2.

The second part of the headline, "what a photographer found in one cubic foot", is informative, it tells us what the article will be about. The text is also informative, we learn what the photographer found in "his green-edged metal cube" as we read on. The headline adds to the effectiveness of the text because it shows that readers will learn something new from the article.

The first words of the headline, "all things bright and beautiful" give us a clue about what the photographer has found — lots of bright and beautiful things, which add to the reader's curiosity.

The image immediately connects with the headline because it's a picture of lots of bright and beautiful creatures in a small space. But to find out that the creatures in the photograph are some of the reef life from French Polynesia, we need to read the text. So the image makes the reader interested to learn more from the article.

First sentence goes straight into answering the question.

This links the headline with the effectiveness of the text.

Shows effect of the image.

This B grade answer starts to show how the <u>headline</u>, <u>image</u> and <u>text work together</u> to get the reader's <u>interest</u>. It needs more <u>detail</u> and <u>examples</u> to get better marks though.

Grade A & A* Answers to Question 2

You need to show you Understand the Effect of the Image and Headline

1) <u>Plan</u> your answer so that it's <u>well organised</u> and <u>flows well</u>.

2) Use <u>examples</u> and give <u>detailed explanations</u> of your points.

This is an <u>"A" grade</u> answer to question 2.

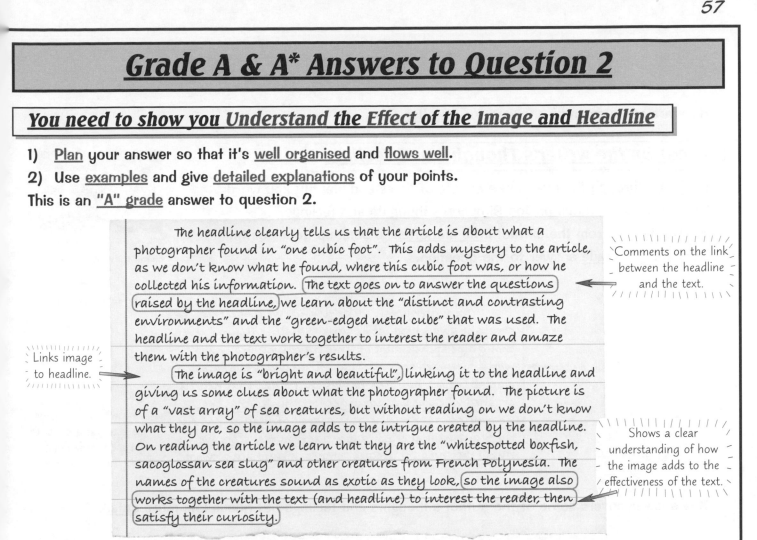

The headline clearly tells us that the article is about what a photographer found in "one cubic foot". This adds mystery to the article, as we don't know what he found, where this cubic foot was, or how he collected his information. The text goes on to answer the questions raised by the headline, we learn about the "distinct and contrasting environments" and the "green-edged metal cube" that was used. The headline and the text work together to interest the reader and amaze them with the photographer's results.
The image is "bright and beautiful", linking it to the headline and giving us some clues about what the photographer found. The picture is of a "vast array" of sea creatures, but without reading on we don't know what they are, so the image adds to the intrigue created by the headline. On reading the article we learn that they are the "whitespotted boxfish, sacoglossan sea slug" and other creatures from French Polynesia. The names of the creatures sound as exotic as they look, so the image also works together with the text (and headline) to interest the reader, then satisfy their curiosity.

Comments on the link between the headline and the text.

Links image to headline.

Shows a clear understanding of how the image adds to the effectiveness of the text.

This answer shows a <u>clear</u>, <u>detailed understanding</u> of the <u>effect</u> of the <u>headline and image</u>.

An A* Answer should be Fluent and Well Structured

1) You should include lots of <u>detailed evidence</u> to <u>back up</u> your points.

2) Use <u>technical terms</u> and focus on the <u>effect</u> on the reader.

Here's an <u>"A*" grade</u> answer to the question.

This shows you're really thinking about the subtle effect of the headline.

Good use of short quotes incorporated into the answer.

This really develops the point — good use of P.E.E.D.

Good conclusion to summarise the answer.

The headline of this article introduces the main idea of the text: that a photographer has found an "astonishing amount" of life in one cubic foot. It begins with the first line of a hymn: "all things bright and beautiful", which famously continues "all creatures great and small". This idea is echoed throughout the article as "creatures as big as a racoon and as small as a leopard slug" were all found in the photographer's "12-inch metal frame". The second part of the headline, "what a photographer found in one cubic foot" creates interest by raising questions about what the photographer found and how he did it. These questions can only be answered by reading the text, so the headline works to attract readers to the informative text.
The image reinforces the effect of the headline, as it shows a "vast array" of "bright and beautiful" sea creatures. The animals are so small and colourful that they look more like jewellery than sea creatures. This supports the text in which the photographer uses a simile to describe the results of his experiment as "like finding little gems". This description makes the creatures seem precious, rare and beautiful, which adds to the interest and intrigue created by the headline.
The overall effect of the image and headline is to capture the reader's attention and make them want to read the rest of the article. They also emphasise the main idea of the article: that there is an amazing "diversity and abundance of life" in just a small space.

Grade C & B Answers to Question 3

Here are some example answers for <u>question 3</u>.

Focus on the writer's Thoughts and Feelings

1) <u>Read through</u> the question a couple of times and identify <u>key words</u>.
2) You need to focus on Joe Simpson's <u>thoughts</u> and <u>feelings</u>.
3) <u>Quote</u> bits from the extract <u>little and often</u> to back up your points.

Here's a <u>"C" grade</u> answer to the question.

Charles found his fear of flying quite embarrassing.

Use your own words — this bit is copied from the text.

> The writer doesn't like flying, we know this straight away because he says "I dislike flying", even though he spends a lot of time travelling around the world. He used to think that "flying was the safest way to travel" but then he was in a plane that nearly crashed when he was younger. He thinks that the near miss is the reason he is scared of flying. When the plane nearly crashed it made him feel sick, we know this because it says "stomach emptying swoop".

Quote supports point.

This would be a good place to put a quote to back up the point.

This answer covers some of the author's thoughts and feelings but needs lots more <u>detail</u>.

Organise your Answer so it's Easy To Follow

1) <u>Plan</u> your answer carefully to make sure it'll really <u>focus</u> on the question you've been asked.
2) It's a good idea to jot down the thoughts and feelings in a quick <u>plan</u> so you can <u>organise</u> them into <u>separate points</u>.

Here's a <u>"B" grade</u> answer to the question.

Good opening — gets straight to the point.

Good use of quotation.

> Joe Simpson describes how he felt happy and confident about flying when he was younger, accepting that it was "the safest way to travel". His feelings about flying changed over time and now he has an "irrational fear" of it. He thinks that his fear of flying developed because of an incident that happened when he was fourteen years old, when the plane he was in narrowly avoided an accident.
> The author's feelings about flying become really clear in his description of the "terrifying landing". Through using words like "suddenly", "screaming" and "frightening" he makes it clear to us that it was a terrifying experience.

Shows interpretation of his feelings from the language used.

This answer begins to go <u>focus</u> well on the question. However, the points need to be <u>developed</u> a bit more to <u>link</u> his feelings about flying to the near miss he had.

Grade A & A* Answers to Question 3

Try and Interpret what the writer says

1) You need to show that you really understand <u>what the writer means</u>.

2) Try and <u>work out</u> what the writer's thoughts and feelings are from the things he says and does.

3) <u>Structure</u> your answer so that it's <u>fluent</u> and <u>easy to follow</u>.

Here's an <u>"A" grade</u> answer to the question.

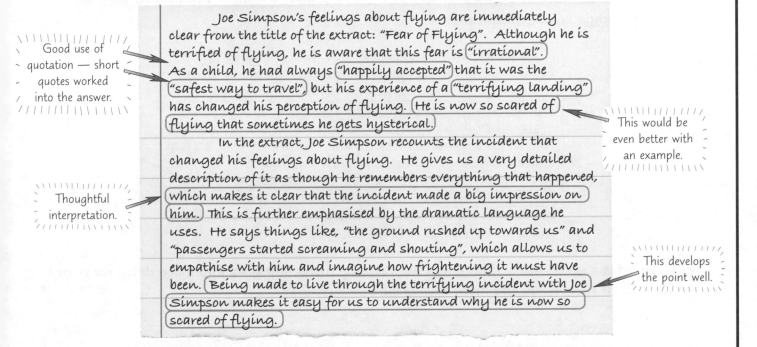

Joe Simpson's feelings about flying are immediately clear from the title of the extract: "Fear of Flying". Although he is terrified of flying, he is aware that this fear is "irrational". As a child, he had always "happily accepted" that it was the "safest way to travel", but his experience of a "terrifying landing" has changed his perception of flying. He is now so scared of flying that sometimes he gets hysterical.

In the extract, Joe Simpson recounts the incident that changed his feelings about flying. He gives us a very detailed description of it as though he remembers everything that happened, which makes it clear that the incident made a big impression on him. This is further emphasised by the dramatic language he uses. He says things like, "the ground rushed up towards us" and "passengers started screaming and shouting", which allows us to empathise with him and imagine how frightening it must have been. Being made to live through the terrifying incident with Joe Simpson makes it easy for us to understand why he is now so scared of flying.

Good use of quotation — short quotes worked into the answer.

This would be even better with an example.

Thoughtful interpretation.

This develops the point well.

Show that you really Understand the author's Thoughts and Feelings

1) Include lots of <u>detailed examples</u> to support the points you're making.

2) Try and think about what the author is <u>implying</u>, as well as what he actually says.

This is an <u>"A*" grade</u> answer to question 3.

Joe Simpson's "Fear of Flying" is made clear in the very first line; he tells us "To put it mildly, I dislike flying". By putting it "mildly" he is ironically understating his feelings to show that he absolutely detests flying. This feeling is made even more clear by the ridiculous situation he recounts where he was "locked in the lavatory" and "in a state close to hysteria" due to his fear of flying. This use of hyperbole contrasts with his understated language, which entertains the reader and leaves them in no doubt that he is terrified of flying.

These feelings contrast sharply with how he thought of flying when he was younger; he used to accept that it was the "safest way to travel" and that his chances of being in an accident were "so small as to be not worth worrying about". He even says that his fear is "irrational", which shows that he knows his fear isn't logical.

He explains where he thinks his fear comes from: a "terrifying landing" he experienced in Germany, aged fourteen. This incident has remained fixed in his mind; he describes the "stomach emptying swoop" and "shocking force" of the landing. These vivid descriptions help us to empathise with his terror and understand his feelings better. He remembers feeling unnerved by "adult males" screaming, as he had previously thought that "men were not supposed to scream". This thought highlights the fact that the near miss altered his perceptions not only of flying, but also of how men are supposed to behave.

This shows you understand the more subtle, implied points.

Confident use of technical terms.

Thoughtful comment.

Really develops the point.

Grade C & B Answers to Question 4

Last question now. Remind yourself of the questions and texts by looking back at pages 46-49.

Make sure you write about Both Texts

1) Read the question <u>a couple of times</u> to make sure you really <u>understand</u> what to do.

2) You need to look for <u>similarities</u> and <u>differences</u> — you're <u>comparing</u> the two texts.

3) Think about <u>who</u> the items are written for — it'll help you to work out what their <u>purpose</u> is.

Here's a <u>"C" grade</u> answer to question 4.

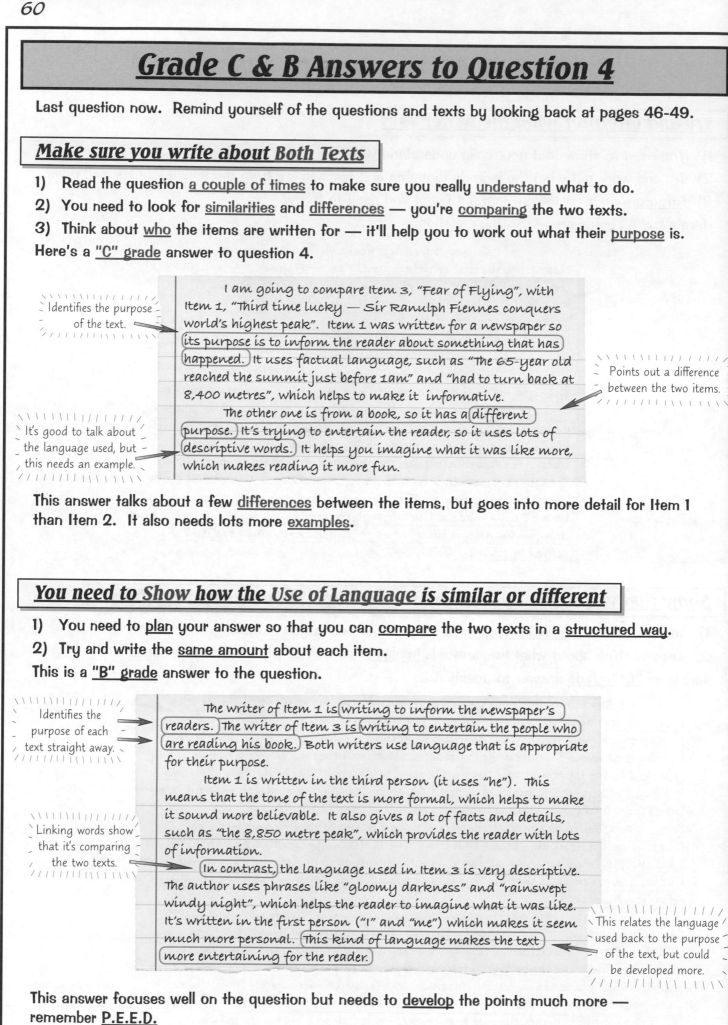

Identifies the purpose of the text.

> I am going to compare Item 3, "Fear of Flying", with Item 1, "Third time lucky — Sir Ranulph Fiennes conquers world's highest peak". Item 1 was written for a newspaper so its purpose is to inform the reader about something that has happened. It uses factual language, such as "The 65-year old reached the summit just before 1am" and "had to turn back at 8,400 metres", which helps to make it informative.
>   The other one is from a book, so it has a different purpose. It's trying to entertain the reader, so it uses lots of descriptive words. It helps you imagine what it was like more, which makes reading it more fun.

Points out a difference between the two items.

It's good to talk about the language used, but this needs an example.

This answer talks about a few <u>differences</u> between the items, but goes into more detail for Item 1 than Item 2. It also needs lots more <u>examples</u>.

You need to Show how the Use of Language is similar or different

1) You need to <u>plan</u> your answer so that you can <u>compare</u> the two texts in a <u>structured way</u>.

2) Try and write the <u>same amount</u> about each item.

This is a <u>"B" grade</u> answer to the question.

Identifies the purpose of each text straight away.

> The writer of Item 1 is writing to inform the newspaper's readers. The writer of Item 3 is writing to entertain the people who are reading his book. Both writers use language that is appropriate for their purpose.
>   Item 1 is written in the third person (it uses "he"). This means that the tone of the text is more formal, which helps to make it sound more believable. It also gives a lot of facts and details, such as "the 8,850 metre peak", which provides the reader with lots of information.
>   In contrast, the language used in Item 3 is very descriptive. The author uses phrases like "gloomy darkness" and "rainswept windy night", which helps the reader to imagine what it was like. It's written in the first person ("I" and "me") which makes it seem much more personal. This kind of language makes the text more entertaining for the reader.

Linking words show that it's comparing the two texts.

This relates the language used back to the purpose of the text, but could be developed more.

This answer focuses well on the question but needs to <u>develop</u> the points much more — remember <u>P.E.E.D.</u>

Grade A & A* Answers to Question 4

Relate each point back to the Writer's Purpose

1) Your answer should show <u>understanding</u> of the effect of <u>language</u> and the <u>purpose</u> of both items.

2) Make good use of <u>quotation</u> to <u>support</u> your points.

Here's an <u>"A" grade</u> answer to the question.

Makes a comparison about purpose straight away.

Shows how the language helps to make the article informative.

Links the language back to the purpose of the article.

> The purpose of Item 1 is to inform the reader, whereas the purpose of Item 3 is to entertain. Item 1 has a factual, formal tone with very little use of emotive language in the article. For example, we are told that Sir Ranulph ran "seven marathons on seven continents" but we don't know anything about how he felt whilst completing them, or indeed his feelings upon summiting Everest. Use of formal language means that readers can take in the information without being distracted by imaginative or emotive descriptions.
>
> On the other hand, Item 3 conveys many of the writer's feelings through descriptive and emotive language. Powerful adjectives like "gloomy" and "shocking", and detailed, imaginative descriptions such as "Suddenly we dropped with a stomach emptying swoop", help the reader imagine what the incident was like. Use of the first person ("I") throughout Item 3 also allows the reader to share Simpson's experience and empathise with him. The more personal and dramatic language used in Item 3 keeps the reader entertained by allowing them to feel closer and more personally involved with the writer's experience.

Write in a Confident, Fluent way

1) Try and include a brief <u>conclusion</u> that sums up your main points.

2) <u>Relate</u> all your points about language to the <u>purpose</u> of the items.

This is an <u>"A*" grade</u> answer to question 4.

Good use of insight.

Good — this links the use of language back to the purpose of the text.

The conclusion neatly summarises the main points.

> Item 1 is a newspaper report which has been written to inform. It uses factual, formal language such as "The 65-year old reached the summit just before 1am (British time)", which makes the article sound more official and informative. However, Item 1 also uses direct speech from Ranulph Fiennes, who is quoted as saying "I won't be returning to Everest", which helps the reader connect to him more personally. This supports the more subtle purpose of the article which is to persuade the reader to "give generously" to Marie Curie Cancer Care.
>
> Conversely, Item 3 is from a non-fiction book and its purpose is to entertain. Unlike Item 1, it's written as a first person narrative (it uses "I" and "we"). This makes the reader feel much more personally involved, as if they are being spoken to by the author. This encourages the reader to engage with the writer, making the text more enjoyable to read.
>
> The writer of Item 1 also uses lots of facts and figures to provide information to the reader; for example, we are told that "in 2008", Fiennes "had to turn back at 8,400 metres". Using facts and figures adds credibility to the article, enabling the reader to trust the article as a source of information.
>
> In contrast to this, Item 3 uses more descriptive language than Item 1, with phrases such as "rainswept windy night". The author also uses other dramatic language techniques such as personification, for example when describing how the plane was "lurching drunkenly". These techniques help the reader to imagine exactly what the situation was like, which makes the text more entertaining because it feels as if you are there with the writer.
>
> In conclusion, the serious, formal language of Item 1 helps the writer to inform the reader, whilst the emotive, dramatic language of Item 3 helps the writer to entertain the reader.

Glossary

alliteration	Where the same sound is repeated at the beginning of words in a phrase. It's often used to make a phrase stand out. E.g. "the <u>b</u>old, <u>b</u>rash <u>b</u>eat of the <u>b</u>and".
analogy	A <u>comparison</u> to show how two things are <u>similar</u>. E.g. "The writer draws an analogy between watching cricket and watching paint dry."
assonance	When words share the same vowel sound, but the consonants are different. E.g. "L<u>i</u>sa had a p<u>ie</u>ce of ch<u>ee</u>se before sh<u>e</u> went to sl<u>ee</u>p, to help her dr<u>ea</u>m."
audience	The people who an author wants to <u>read</u> their writing.
bias	Giving <u>more support</u> to one point of view than to another, due to the writer's <u>own opinions</u> affecting the way they write.
broadsheet	A newspaper with big, <u>long pages</u>, e.g. The Telegraph or The Sunday Times. They're often considered to be more serious and respectable than tabloid newspapers.
byline	A line of text under the headline telling you <u>who's written</u> the article.
caption	A line of text under a photograph or picture, telling you <u>what it shows</u>.
colloquialism	An <u>informal</u> word or phrase that sounds like something said in a <u>conversation</u>. E.g. "Don't keep wittering on about it."
consonants	All the letters in the alphabet that <u>aren't vowels</u>.
context	The <u>background</u> to something, or the situation <u>surrounding</u> it, which affects the way it is written and understood. E.g. "The article was written in the context of the war that was going on."
contrast	When two things are described in a way which emphasises <u>how different</u> they are. E.g. a writer might contrast two different places, or two different attitudes.
counter-argument	A way of arguing a point by first giving the opposite point of view, then <u>disagreeing</u> with it.
emotive language	Language that has an <u>emotional</u> effect on the reader, e.g. making them feel angry.
empathy	When someone feels like they <u>understand</u> what someone else is experiencing and how they <u>feel</u> about it.
exaggeration	Describing something as <u>bigger</u> than it really is. E.g. "A million miles from home".
first person	A personal style of writing, using words like "I", "me", "mine", "we", "us", "our" etc.
font	The style and size of <u>type</u> used.
generalisation	A statement that gives an <u>overall impression</u>, sometimes a misleading one, without going into details. E.g. "Children today eat too much junk food."

Glossary

headline	The statement at the <u>top</u> of a text (e.g. a newspaper article), usually in a <u>large font</u>, used to attract readers' interest by giving an impression of what it's about.
imagery	Language that creates a <u>picture in your mind</u>, bringing the text to life.
implication	When a writer gives an <u>impression</u> that something is the case <u>without</u> saying it outright. E.g. "Last time I left Steve in charge, the house nearly burnt down" — this <u>implies</u> that Steve can't be trusted, without saying it directly.
inconsistency	When one bit of a text <u>contradicts</u> (disagrees with) another bit, so that the argument doesn't really add up. It's a sign of weakness in an argument.
irony	Saying one thing but <u>meaning the opposite</u>. E.g. "What a great idea of mine to go for a nice long walk on the rainiest day of the year."
language	The <u>choice of words</u> used. The language determines the effect the piece of writing will have on the reader, e.g. it can be emotive or persuasive.
layout	The way a piece of writing is visually <u>presented</u> to the reader. E.g. what kind of <u>font</u> is used, whether there are subheadings, the use of photographs, whether text columns are used, and anything else that affects the way a text looks.
media	Any way of <u>communicating</u> with <u>large numbers</u> of people, e.g. newspapers, TV, radio, films, websites, magazines.
metaphor	A way of describing something by saying that it <u>is something else</u>, to create a vivid image. E.g. "His eyes were deep, black, oily pools."
narrative	A part of a text that tells a <u>story</u> or describes an <u>experience</u>.
non-fiction	Writing about the <u>real world</u>, rather than making up a story.
onomatopoeia	A word that <u>sounds like</u> what it's supposed to mean. E.g. "buzz", "crunch", "bang", "pop", "ding".
personification	A special kind of description where you write about something as if it's a <u>person</u> or animal with thoughts or feelings. E.g. "The sea growled hungrily."
pun	A "play on words" — a word or phrase that's deliberately used because it has <u>more than one meaning</u>. E.g. "She lies on the couch at the psychiatrist's", where "lies" could mean "lies down" or "tells lies".
purpose	The <u>reason</u> someone writes a text. E.g. to persuade, to argue, to advise.
rhetoric	<u>Language</u> techniques that are designed to achieve a specific <u>effect</u>, e.g. repetition or exaggeration to make a speech more persuasive.
rhetorical question	A question which <u>doesn't need an answer</u>. E.g. "Are we really expected to put up with this government's lies?"

64

Glossary

sarcasm	Saying something in a cutting, <u>nasty</u> way, often using <u>irony</u>. E.g. "Well done Kerry, another failed exam, you really are a bright spark."
satire	A text that makes fun out of someone, or something, in an attempt to <u>damage their reputation</u>. It's often done by imitating someone and exaggerating their flaws.
simile	A way of describing something by <u>comparing</u> it to something else, usually by using the words "like" or "as". E.g. "He was as pale as the moon," or "Her hair was like a bird's nest."
slang	Words or phrases that sound <u>informal</u> or <u>conversational</u>, e.g. "bloke", "telly", "stop going on about it".
stereotype	An inaccurate, <u>generalised</u> view of a particular <u>group of people</u>. E.g. a stereotype of football fans might be that they're all hooligans.
strapline	A short statement <u>under the headline</u> that gives <u>more information</u> about what the following article is about. The text is smaller than the main headline.
structure	The <u>order</u> and <u>arrangement</u> of a piece of writing. E.g. how the text begins, develops and ends, whether it uses subheadings or not, etc.
style	The <u>way</u> a text is <u>written</u>, e.g. the type of language and techniques used.
subheading	A word or phrase that <u>stands out</u> from the text and <u>divides</u> the text into chunks. It gives an idea of what the <u>next section</u> of text is about.
syllable	A single <u>unit of sound</u> within a word. E.g. "all" has one syllable, "always" has two and "establishmentarianism" has nine.
tabloid	A newspaper with <u>short</u>, almost square pages, e.g. The Sun or The Mirror, often thought of as less serious than broadsheets.
text	Any piece of <u>writing</u>, e.g. an article, a speech, a leaflet.
text formatting	Ways of making bits of text <u>stand out</u>, e.g. **bold**, *italic*, <u>underlining</u>, CAPITALS.
theme	An <u>idea</u> or <u>topic</u> that's important in a piece of writing. E.g. a newspaper article could be based on the theme of third world debt.
tone	The <u>mood</u> of a piece of writing, e.g. happy, sad, serious, lighthearted. It's an overall effect, created by things like choice of words, imagery and layout.
vocabulary	The range of <u>words</u> used by a writer or in a specific text.
voice	The <u>personality</u> of the writer of a text. It can be fairly neutral, as in some broadsheet newspaper articles, or very opinionated, like in a tabloid editorial.
vowels	Simple — the letters '<u>a</u>', '<u>e</u>', '<u>i</u>', '<u>o</u>' and '<u>u</u>' (and sometimes 'y', e.g. in "happy").

Index

Index

Index

Acknowledgements

The Publisher would like to thank the following copyright holders for permission to reproduce texts and images:

Article on page 48 entitled 'All things bright and beautiful: what a photographer found in one cubic foot', Copyright Guardian News & Media Ltd 2010.

Image of sea creatures on page 48, David Liittschwager/National Geographic Stock.

Extract on page 49 entitled 'Fear of Flying' from *Storms of Silence* by Joe Simpson. Published by Vintage Books. Reprinted by permission of the Random House Group Ltd.

Every effort has been made to locate copyright holders and obtain permission to reproduce texts and images. For those texts and images where it has been difficult to trace the originator of the work, we would be grateful for information. If any copyright holder would like us to make an amendment to the acknowledgements, please notify us and we will gladly update the book at the next reprint. Thank you.